"One restless woman from America seeking—*something* . . . and one homeless boy from Africa seeking—*someone* . . . write a story that has your heart colliding with what you're looking for—right where you are."

—**Ann Voskamp**, author of the *New York Times* bestseller
One Thousand Gifts

"This book isn't just a story, it's an invitation to love extravagantly. It's the voices of Sammy and Claire telling us that the power of God's love trumps our fears and circumstances. It's about relentless hope and tremendous love. Buckle up, you're about to be changed."

—**Bob Goff**, Honorary Consul for the Republic of Uganda;
New York Times bestselling author of *Love Does*

"Claire knows firsthand what it means to really give of her time and talent, and in this book she challenged me to do the same. What a brave step of faith she took—and continues to live. My heart sings that there are people in the world like her."

—**Tsh Oxenreider**, author of *Notes from a Blue Bike*

"This is a beautiful story, beautifully told. I could read Sammy's and Claire's stories for days on end. This book is a timely reminder that love and hope can bridge continents and create family anywhere."

—**Shauna Niequist**, author of *Bread & Wine*

"If you're looking for a life that matters, if you're craving something you can't quite put your finger on, maybe start with this book. And the story of how extraordinary sometimes looks nothing like climbing Everest but everything like quietly connecting with one person's story. And watching how yours multiplies into something that satisfies way beyond check marks on a bucket list. Claire and Sammy invite us into their story with the comfortable familiarity of old friends, challenging us to see beyond the borders of what we thought life was supposed to hold and how detours are often the best storylines of all."

—**Lisa-Jo Baker**, author of *Surprised by Motherhood*;
community manager for (in)courage

"*Hope Runs* is a powerful reminder of what God can do if we obediently listen to him. Claire is a change maker, has lots of influence, and runs in influential circles, but she still makes sure to focus on what is most important. This book is timely, heartfelt, and honest. I appreciate the grace, hope, love, and adventure lived out through this journey, and now you get to experience it as well!"

—**Brad Lomenick**, president of Catalyst;
author of *The Catalyst Leader*

"I read *Hope Runs* in two days (and I am not a fast reader). I can't think of a more unlikely pair than Sammy and Claire—yet somehow, after reading their story, I can't imagine one separate from the other. Theirs is a powerful, unforgettable story, and I'm truly grateful for their willingness to tell it."

—**Emily P. Freeman**, author of *A Million Little Ways*

"*Hope Runs* is a beautifully moving and heartfelt story of how two lives were completely rearranged by hope and love."

—**Crystal Paine**, founder of MoneySavingMom.com;
author of *Say Goodbye to Survival Mode*

"Claire Díaz-Ortiz has always led with wisdom and heart, and this book is no exception. In her and Sammy's story we have a powerful witness of what happens when we learn to be sensitive to God's voice and step out boldly in faith. *Hope Runs* inspired me and gave me hope; I know it will do the same for readers around the country."

—**Joshua DuBois**, author of *The President's Devotional*;
founder of Values Partnerships; former executive director
of the White House faith-based initiative

"Claire and Sammy are two lovely people who tell their story of hope with such incredibly moving authenticity. This book will inspire you!"

—**Alli Worthington**, strategist, speaker, and author

"*Hope Runs* brings the feeling of a downhill sprint: your heart will pound, your spirit will rise, and you'll be caught up in the rush that comes from stepping out in faith and letting life run away with you."

—**Scott Williams**, church growth/leadership consultant
and strategist at Nxt Level Solutions;
author of *Church Diversity* and *Go Big*

"Sammy and Claire share a powerful story of two lives changed and challenge us to listen for God's voice and bravely step out in faith."

—**Rebekah Lyons**, cofounder of Q Ideas;
author of *Freefall to Fly*

"Stories of overcoming impossible obstacles move me, but *Hope Runs* did more: it changed my cynicism to hope. I dare to believe that people who are hurt in and by this world can rise above and run a new, life-changing race. Sammy's voice and Claire's story reminded me of everything good about the human spirit."

—**Mary DeMuth**, author of *The Wall Around Your Heart*

HOPE RUNS

An American Tourist, a Kenyan Boy, a Journey of Redemption

Claire Díaz-Ortiz and
Samuel Ikua Gachagua

Revell

a division of Baker Publishing Group
Grand Rapids, Michigan

Published by Revell
a division of Baker Publishing Group
P.O. Box 6287, Grand Rapids, MI 49516-6287
www.revellbooks.com

Printed in the United States of America

Library of Congress Cataloging-in-Publication Data is on file at the Library of Congress, Washington, DC.

ISBN 978-0-8007-2279-1 (cloth)
ISBN 978-0-8007-2347-7 (ITPE)

Scripture quotations are from the Holy Bible, New International Version®. NIV®. Copyright © 1973, 1978, 1984, 2011 by Biblica, Inc.™ Used by permission of Zondervan. All rights reserved worldwide. www.zondervan.com

To protect the privacy of those who have shared their stories with the authors, some details and names have been changed. For ease of reading, some events have been simplified or condensed.

14 15 16 17 18 19 20   7 6 5 4 3 2 1

In keeping with biblical principles of creation stewardship, Baker Publishing Group advocates the responsible use of our natural resources. As a member of the Green Press Initiative, our company uses recycled paper when possible. The text paper of this book is composed in part of post-consumer waste.

green press INITIATIVE

———⚜———

To all the children in this book and all the
children in orphanages like this one.

And to Lara.

———⚜———

CONTENTS

Contents

SUDAN

ETHIOPIA

UGANDA

KENYA

SOMALIA

Nanyuki

Nakuru

Mount
Kenya

Nyeri

NAIROBI

TANZANIA

INDIAN
OCEAN

0   100   200km
0   100   200ml

José Díaz-Ortiz

FOREWORD

Years ago a therapist friend taught me how to listen. She said when I'm talking to somebody about a painful or sensitive situation, I should sit and listen and then repeat back to them what I heard, making sure I got it right. My therapist friend said this will give the person I'm listening to a sense of comfort, a sense of being known. She said people connect when they take time for empathy.

Reading *Hope Runs* is like sitting down listening to Claire Díaz-Ortiz repeat everything she knows about her foster son. It's her way of saying, "Do I understand you? Do I have your story right? Is this who you are?"

I loved especially reading Claire talk about herself from Sammy's perspective. I loved that Sammy lays in his bed in the orphanage at night hoping Claire won't be like so many of the other white women who only come for a visit then leave forever. And I loved how he discovers that for him, she will become so much more.

I loved the scene where Sammy gets on the plane, the story of him not knowing what a boarding pass is, and then finally getting on the massive building with wings, falling asleep from exhaustion and waking up in Dubai, of how trusting he is as he gets lost in the airport, and how delighted he is to finally be reunited with Claire. But always, always through this book the reader has a haunting sense we're listening to a story we were never intended to hear. It's really about Sammy and about Claire, his new guardian not much older than him, his new friend. And you can hear her whispering to herself as she types, "Is this you, Sammy? Am I understanding your story correctly?"

I know Claire well, and she's more comfortable sitting quietly at a table letting other people talk than she is being the center of attention. And so reading this book let me know what was really going through her head. And what was going through her head was a remarkable consideration for the life of another.

Hope Runs is more than a book, it's a monument to empathy. I'm grateful to have been able to eavesdrop on this private conversation, a retelling of a life as a way to connect Claire to Sammy first, then the rest of us to them. Connection through empathy indeed.

—Donald Miller
Author of *Blue Like Jazz*

SAMMY

CHAPTER 1

I was born on a red dirt road.

It was a hot December in Limuru, Kenya, and my mother, father, and brother traveled for days to reach my grandmother's house for Christmas. On December 23, 1992, my mother gave birth.

They call me Sammy.

My mother, father, brother, and I live in Nakuru, a big, mile-high town in the west of Kenya, where there is white dirt as far as the eye can see. My father is a businessman who manages an insurance company. I remember him coming home from work with my mother one day. I am bursting with joy at seeing him, and I run and run and run to hug him. At that moment, I feel I can run forever.

This is the best memory I have of my father.

When I am a small boy, our family is very successful. My mother's sister lives in our house, working as our maid, cooking for us, and taking care of my brother and me.

We eat chicken every day. In Kenya, when you eat chicken, you are successful.

When I am four or five, my mother tells me it is time for me to start school. I don't understand what school is, but I am happy for a new checked shirt and a bright red sweater. That first day my mother takes my hand and walks me along the white dirt road of the Nakuru plains. By the time I get to school, the shoes I had shined sparkling black are now full of dust.

At school, I am confused. It doesn't make sense to me that I am to stay an entire day in a new place, an entire day without my mother. This I cannot comprehend.

That same year my mother starts getting fat. I don't know why until she sits my brother and me down to tell us she is expecting a baby.

I am happy. "Finally we're buying another person for the family!" I shout.

All that my mother says at first is, "No, Sammy, we are not buying a baby." She says she is going to give birth. But that doesn't make sense to me, and I tell her I have always believed that people are bought, and that the reason I have an older brother is because my parents purchased him somewhere.

My mother tries to make me grasp the truth, explaining that sometimes when people love each other they can make babies.

I do not understand one bit, and we leave it at that.

It is around this time that my father gets sick and goes to the hospital. They tell me he has a very bad headache and the doctor needs to take care of him. A few days later something strange happens. My mother says she and my father are getting married that same week, on Saturday. I am small and don't think about the fact that they were not married before.

"While he's in hospital?" I ask.

It doesn't make any sense to me.

First we have a ceremony in the church, but my father can't come to that. Then we go to the hospital and there is another ceremony just for him. People peer in through the bars of the hospital window to see.

At the wedding, there are many cars. I have never seen so many cars before, and I want so badly to ride in one because I never have. Someone is carrying around a strange machine, and I want to know what it is. My cousin tells me it is a camera. "You know how you see videos on the TV? Well, that thing records the videos that go there!" he says.

That seems to me the greatest thing in the world. I don't have a chance to touch it, but I keep it in my mind and hope that someday I can.

One Tuesday morning in 1997 we get a beautiful sister named Elizabeth, whom we call Bethi. It is a wonderful day. My mom receives many presents, and we make gallons of uji, a drink of watery maize meal that I have a special taste for.

That night both my dad and my mom are in the same hospital together, and everyone is happy.

The next day, on Wednesday, I wake up at home and am getting ready to go back to the hospital to see my baby sister and my parents when dozens of people start rushing into our house, talking in hushed tones. Some people are crying, and I see my cousin fall to the floor with tears in her eyes. When I ask what is happening, she tells me.

My father has passed away.

As I try to understand what that means, my brother says that I will never see my father again. He's gone for good, he says.

But that—that is something I cannot believe.

This is the beginning of a horrible day. We go to the hospital, and when we are there I see my father's mother, whom I don't remember ever meeting before. She is old and bent over and walks with a cane.

One week later, another Wednesday, we bury my father in an orange casket in a public cemetery, and I see my mother cry for the first time. I still don't understand what death is, but I cry with her. I have a picture of me from this day, the day my father died. It is one of the only pictures I have of my life in Kenya.

After my father's death, things start to go downhill for our family. At first my mother continues to work as a land broker, and we keep on living in the big, busy town of Nakuru.

During this time, I come to love making tea. Kenyan tea, or chai, is made of boiled water mixed with milk, sugar, and special black tea. One rainy Friday afternoon I get home and find my mother and her friend Jadi inside cracking jokes and laughing loud. I go to the kitchen and make tea for them. Jadi tells me she has never had better tea, and I smile wide. As I wash their dishes, though, I hear their voices start to rise. Soon they are shouting. When the shouting doesn't stop and my mother chases Jadi out of the house, I know we have lost a friend. Jadi isn't the only friend my mother loses, and she starts getting in fights with many people who have been in our lives for a long time.

Later that night our mom calls us out of our rooms to come sit on her bed with her. My little sister Bethi is in the crib as we crowd around my mother, praying over a Bible. My mother has never been much of a churchgoer, and we only go every now and then. She certainly doesn't pray much in front of us. That night, though, she prays hard. And then she starts to cry. This is the second time I have seen her cry, and this time I do not know why.

After my mother tells us she has lost her job, we start moving. We change houses, get kicked out of one house, rent another, and get kicked out again. One time we move to a house that is close to my primary school. We are there a few weeks when kids around the neighborhood start to get chicken pox. At first we don't get it. But our luck doesn't last for long, and two days later it happens. Muriithi, my brother, is the first, and he passes it on to me. When little Bethi gets it, she is covered in spots. She has a hole in her hand from the spots, and we put fifteen drops of medicine in the hole each day to make it go away. We do this again and again.

Little by little, my sister starts healing. Right at that time, though, my mother's sister Veronica, who has been cleaning for us, starts acting strangely. She is sleeping a lot for no reason and wanders around the house not doing anything. She doesn't even have the energy to beat us much! Then, a few months later, she gives birth to a baby boy. I am surprised, but then I am happy when she names him after our grandfather and me: Sammy Ikua.

Growing up with baby Ikua, even though we live together less than a year, is wonderful. It is quite a change from having a little sister to having a little brother. And even though he is just an infant, I feel responsible in a new way.

I love being a big brother to Bethi and baby Ikua, and whenever we get kicked out of school for not paying school fees, I come home and play with baby Ikua and swing him around. Veronica, however, is back to treating us terribly and beating us for everything. One time Muriithi gets a paper cut and she beats him thoroughly.

Even though my mother loves visitors, Veronica hates them and never lets us bring friends home. One day I don't listen and bring one with me. She beats me very badly, and I never bring anyone home ever again while I live with her.

As time goes by and my mom still doesn't have a job, Veronica has to leave because my mother can't pay to keep her anymore. The night she leaves, Muriithi, Bethi, and I have a little party because we are so happy she has finally gone away. As we watch TV, Bethi laughs for the first time, a small chuckle.

I scream at once and run to call my brother. "Bethi's laughing! Bethi's laughing!" Then I go to my mother and tell her the same thing. Even though I know it has something to do with the TV, I convince myself otherwise. "She's laughing because Veronica is finally out of the house!" I say.

Once again I feel lucky. But the next day we go to school, and the teacher makes us leave because we haven't paid school fees for over a year.

Even though we don't have money and keep getting kicked out of school, I always feel our mother loves us. One time I go to school the day after I have just been kicked out. The head teacher who made me leave the day before isn't there, and I think, *Yes! I can stay in class today!* But as soon as I get to the classroom, the classroom teacher demands that I pay her. When I tell her I don't have any money, she begins shouting louder and louder. Then she picks up a stick and begins beating me on my thighs.

I cry over my hurting legs as I walk home and wait for my mother. When she sees what has happened, she is furious. The next morning we wake up very early and she takes me by the hand back to the school, where I watch her yell at the teacher, saying that she cannot do this to a little boy. I am grateful, but I do think it is a little funny, because my mother has done this very thing before.

Early one Saturday morning my mother sends my brother to buy mandazi, the Kenyan doughnuts we all love. He is taking forever to come back, and eventually I walk over to the factory where they make the doughnuts to ask if anyone has seen a small boy. The man tells me they've seen a lot of small boys this morning, so how is he supposed to know which one I'm talking about?

I go home and my mother sends me to the mandazi store, where I ask the same question. "Have you seen a little boy who came in to buy six mandazi?" They also tell me the place has been full of little boys!

My mother is starting to get very worried, and a few hours later she calls her friend, who tries to calm her down. At midday, when Muriithi still isn't back, my mother gets a group of friends together to start looking for him. We also go to the police station, where my mother cries as she begs the officers to help her.

All day we search for Muriithi, but we cannot find him. That evening, we come back home and everyone stands in the house praying together for his return. As we are praying, we see Muriithi walking slowly up to the house, leaning on a stick. He seems exhausted and says that he had been taken and beaten by bad men. My mother is very worried but begins thanking God again and again. She gives Muriithi a bath and some food and we all go to bed. My mother doesn't stop praising God for his safe return.

A few weeks later one of our cousins comes to visit. After we greet one another and give her some tea, she asks how Muriithi is doing. We didn't think she had heard about what happened, so we are confused why she is asking. Then she explains that one Saturday several weeks back she found Muriithi asleep in the town's stadium. He told her he was tired and not feeling well and that he had stayed in the stadium all day.

Later that night Muriithi tells my mother the truth. After he bought the mandazi doughnuts that Saturday morning, he lost the ten shillings in change he received. He was scared of my mother's reaction—the last time he lost change, she beat him badly—and decided to pretend that he was kidnapped and beaten.

My mother listens calmly and tells him she is sad he lied, but he doesn't need to do what he did. "If anything ever happens to you, you shouldn't worry," she says. "We are a family, and you can come back and we can always talk about things. Yes, there might be consequences, but I would never do anything really bad to you."

My mother doesn't get a new job, but over the next few years she does get new friends. These are people I have never met before, and some of them are very pretty. They dress very well and always look good in their short skirts. Around this time, my mother starts getting male friends as well.

I remember her first one, Boniface. He seems to always be in our house, especially on Friday nights. The first Friday night that he comes, he doesn't leave when we go to bed, and on Saturday morning he is still there. When we get up, he gives us money to go buy Blue Band, the margarine we love, and bread and tea. It is the best breakfast we have had in a long time, and we don't think anymore about where he slept the night before.

We all adore Boniface. Muriithi especially loves him, and that's when he decides to take his name. Since that day everyone but me has always called my brother Boniface.

One day Boniface comes by with a car and teaches my mother how to drive. Another day he comes and brings us mandazi dough-nuts. On a different day he gives us twenty shillings each, and we could not be happier. But then Boniface stops coming, and my mother doesn't say what has happened to him.

After Boniface leaves, there is another man, Jimmy, who I don't like at all. One Monday morning I oversleep and don't wake up in time for school. I am in the second or third grade at the time, and when I do finally wake up, I see that Muriithi is already gone. My mother, who tells us she has to leave at night now to go do the work she has found, still isn't home. I take a shower in the yard in a bucket, as usual, and am getting ready for school when I realize how late it is. Given the time, I decide not to bother with school, and instead I leave the house and spend the day walking around the streets, not wanting to go home in case my mother finds me there.

I am waiting for Muriithi to get out of school so I can walk home with him and my mother will think I have been in school, when I run into Jimmy on the streets. He asks how I am and then asks after my mother. I tell him she is good and that she went to work the night before.

When I say that she went to work, his face falls. I don't know what that means, as I thought work was a good thing, but then Jimmy asks if I want a soda. He buys me one—and a piece of cake!—and I eat it all up so happily. Meanwhile, he walks over to the phone booth nearby and puts some coins in. When the person on the other end of the line picks up, I hear him start singing a famous Swahili song, and then he hangs up.

When I am done with my soda, I thank Jimmy and go home.

At home, I find Muriithi already there, and he immediately asks where I have been. "I was in school," I lie. "I just stayed in the classroom so you didn't see me." But he doesn't believe me and tells me he came to the classroom to check. "I was in school!" I swear in a louder voice.

When my mother comes home, she also asks me questions. "Where were you today?"

I tell her the same thing I told Muriithi and expand on my story. "We had math, we had English, and all the other classes."

Then she tells me her friend Jimmy called her. "Why were you with him?" she asks. I tell her I met him on the way home, but she doesn't believe me. "Sammy, he said he saw you before school got out. Did you go to school today?"

I don't know what to say, and so I finally tell the truth.

She gets a pipe and tells me to lie down. She hits me with two strokes on my backside. I don't have pants on, and it hurts very badly. She gives me another two strokes, and then two more. Then she tells me to never, never skip school again.

Since that day I have never skipped school.

The first time my mother is jailed, she spends two days there. She tells the police it's not her fault and that if they don't believe her they can go talk to her husband. "If you want to speak to him, you can go to his grave," she says.

They let her go.

Then she is jailed a second time, this time for four days.

One morning I wake up and my mother hasn't come home from whatever work she does at night. We go to school as usual, though, and there is a big footrace for all the students. I win the race that day, and they give me an orange jacket as a prize. It is a little too big for me, but I am happy.

After school, Muriithi and I go to pick up our sister from the nursery and then go home. We watch TV until the lights turn off. That is when we realize that our mother must not have paid the light bill. But the jacket they gave me at school came with a candle inside! So we use it to get ready for bed. And even though we go to bed that night without eating and aren't sure where our mother is, finding that candle makes me feel that God is up there looking out for us.

The next day, since we have no food in the house, we ask to borrow food from the shop near our house.

We are worried about our mother and don't know what is happening, so we stay home from school. For three days we stay home, waiting for the lights, borrowing food from the shop, and looking for our mother. On the fifth day our mother comes back, and we are so glad to see her we want to cry. She tells us what happened, but I don't understand her words, and I only hear when she congratulates us that we thought to borrow food. We feel smart and happy.

I know things are getting hard for my mother when she starts staying up all night, asking me to sit and pray with her, putting our hands on the Bible. The worst days are the days when the landlord comes around asking for payment. Sometimes she hides. "Tell him I'm not in the house," she says. And we say she is gone.

Every now and then I see my mother crying for no reason. Even though we are hungry, I am glad we are together.

One Tuesday night we are all sitting together with our hands on the Bible, praying. Even my four-year-old sister's hands are on the book as my mother says that she has finally found a good job in the capital city of Nairobi. She is leaving the next day, she tells us.

The capital! I am amazed. We cannot contain our happiness. I truly believe we have never felt so happy. All our problems will go away! We can go to school every day without getting kicked out and eat every night!

After she tells us she will leave tomorrow, she mentions that she will be visiting us every Wednesday. We are so thrilled that this doesn't register with us. We don't ask how we are going to live by ourselves, or feed ourselves, or do everything without her throughout the whole week.

The next day she leaves early in the morning, and we go to school as normal.

That first Wednesday she leaves us with two hundred shillings, and that first Thursday we use one hundred shillings without thinking. And then on Friday, like normal kids, we waste the other one hundred shillings. On Saturday we don't have any more money, but we don't worry because she is coming back on Wednesday.

On Wednesday, though, she doesn't come.

When we start to get worried, we tell ourselves that maybe she couldn't come for some reason, but she will be back the next Wednesday.

It is only one week more, we say to ourselves.

By the next Wednesday our mother still hasn't returned, and our neighbors begin to ask us, "What's happened? Where's your mother?"

We say, "Oh, she has work in Nairobi, but she'll be back next Wednesday." We say it again and again and again to everyone who asks.

But she never shows up. Not once does my mother ever again appear.

CLAIRE

CHAPTER 2

By the time I finally got to Africa, I had the notion that I already knew her. Years of thumbing through thick memoirs and ratty guide-books extolling her magic had given me the sense that I understood the secrets held in her heavy air and fierce green trees. But when I did arrive and saw how the red dirt seeps into you in ways that will never leave, I realized, of course, that I never knew anything at all.

But this story is getting ahead of me.

First there was Mexico.

I went to Mexico because a bad book told me to.

While spending six months studying in Italy during college, I developed a perhaps unnatural love for a particular bookstore and frequented the place on a near daily basis. One day a colorful book about Mexico caught my eye, and I bought it without even reading the back cover.

Months later I began to read. The book chronicled the story of a middle-aged Californian couple's experiences living south of the border. Lots of typically quirky things happened that I found mildly inane. They had trouble with contractors. They started talking to each other in Spanish. They learned to love the local dogs. Although I found little common ground with the writer, I made the decision to go.

It would take two years to tie up loose ends—friends, family, and school—in California, and I looked forward to the change.

I had been born and raised in Northern California's Berkeley and had spent my high school years at the enormous Berkeley High School, where the drug deals that took place in first period, and the bathroom monitors who ensured we didn't use our bathroom breaks to add to the school's virulent problem with arson, always ran in sharp contrast to my summers spent at a placid Christian camp. College at Stanford University was another shock to my system, and I remember stopping in wonder when I heard the rumor shortly after arriving that each of the hundreds of palm trees dotting Stanford's Palm Drive had cost the university fifty thousand dollars to fly in from a far-off place.

I loved the incredible academic environment and opportunities at Stanford fiercely, and when I finished my undergraduate studies in just under three years, I decided to stay on for four to complete a master's degree and graduate with my dear friends and boyfriend. In the process, though, I pushed myself too hard by doubling up on classes and holding two part-time jobs, and for more than a year I was ill. An autoimmune disorder appeared to be the culprit, leading me to sleep thirteen hours a day and regularly retreat from the world with unbearable migraines.

I longed for a place and time where my life could come to a standstill—at least for a while. I want to be *bored*, I said.

By going too fast for too long, I had worn myself out and knew that I needed to make a drastic change to attempt to begin anew. Somehow I felt that by physically leaving California, I could give myself the space to find open air again. I needed to breathe.

The month before I left, another book invaded. This time I specifically remembered a particular Mexican travelogue I had read years ago, and I went hunting for it to learn more about this country I was off to. When I found it, in a dark and smelly section of a California library, I could tell it was the exact copy I had taken out years before. As I opened it, the first sentence startled me. It really wasn't even mildly jarring, but I can be a little too excitable. "There are only two ways to get to San Miguel," it read.

I had already decided to move to San Miguel.

One month later my plane lands in Mexico, and although I had attempted to pack light, the number of add-ons to my luggage had grown enormously in the past few weeks. As I drag my suitcases through customs, the official asks me what a muffin tin is doing sticking out of the side of my bag. Fatigued from two days of travel—a remarkable feat considering it should have been only a four-hour flight—I look at him quizzically. "It won't fit," I explain.

The airport shuttle is full of American tourists coming to San Miguel for various purposes. A woman behind me explains she had a midlife crisis at twenty-seven and became a flight attendant so she could spend all her weekends in San Miguel instead of Philadelphia. An overweight woman in town for a wedding explains the upcoming procedure she will have when she returns to Texas—something one step short of a gastric bypass. An L.A. comedian is here to study with a prominent teacher of humor.

When they ask what I am doing here, I explain as vaguely and as well as I can. "I am moving here," I say.

"Really?" they ask, intrigued. "Why?"

"I'm not entirely certain," I say, and then the questions come screaming in like those of other people's parents at a bad college graduation party. What will you do? Where will you live? How long will you stay? The comedian discusses what an inspiring thing it is to pack up and just *go* somewhere, and she begins talking about a book she read on some woman who moved to Africa at the turn of the century.

I want to tell her that I have read nearly every book that exists about Western women who run off to live in Africa, and every single one of those women had something strong in them that I do not have. Instead, I say simply, "I am not that person."

The thin roads wind in and out of the hills, and I massage my wrists to keep the nausea at bay. I know little about San Miguel de Allende, but what I do know has much to do with the strange international crowd it has coerced into living there. It is a favorite artsy getaway for expatriates, and the American population has soared in recent years thanks to a large expat retiree community.

But I am not coming to San Miguel to retire. Instead, I am coming to work as an anthropologist with international volunteers at an organization that has offered me a cubbyhole to try out a new model I developed in graduate school. In the particular field I study, I am interested in international volunteer programs, where Westerners embark on excursions to save the world only to realize along the way that they are learning far more from the experience than the locals, who are often confused about why the Westerners came in the first place.

This is the premise of my work: very little can be accomplished in short-term English teaching programs (which usually involve unqualified teachers) and passing-out-toothbrush health programs (which usually involve unqualified health workers). Instead, the way to enact true social change in the world is to acknowledge that the biggest impact at work is often not in the conversational English skills or hygiene needs of the local populations but rather in the volunteer's own transformation. If it was really all about the locals, after all, many times we'd be much better off sending our money to organizations that employ locals on the ground to do the English teaching and the health work.

However, by having one cross-cultural experience, then another and another, these volunteers—if given the right tools to recognize the importance of what they themselves are actually learning—have a good chance of one day doing something that can hopefully make things a little better. The volunteer's value to the local is not in that single three-month stint building a church or two but in the possibility that those three months can transform the volunteer into someone who gives for life. My work is about helping organizations see this and making their programming more sustainable in the process.

In Mexico, I hope to use these skills.

I will always remember the moment when I realize the van has crossed into San Miguel. Still rubbing my wrists to stave off nausea, I watch the flight attendant point excitedly down a mediocre-looking street and say something monumental like, "That is where I lived for four months!" Meanwhile, I am looking around and thinking that this place is not at all what I had been envisioning. The streets seem too small, nothing looks very charming, and there is a lot of unnecessary, suspiciously Mexican-looking dust. I had planned for several years to come here, and I am now officially underwhelmed.

To add to matters, my carefully carved-out professional plan lasts exactly eleven days. Long enough to determine that the organization I had hoped to work at is a mess of interpersonal politics

I do not want to be anywhere near. I'll find other places to use this work over the years, but not in Mexico.

Instead, what I find there is how to be me.

I have been in Mexico about nine months when my boyfriend of several years calls from his home in California to say that he cannot see our future. It is a short phone call, and it ends it all.

We had started the year in Mexico together—in a sense. When I said that I wanted to move to San Miguel, he had found an opportunity in a different city nine hours away by bus. But as Mexico grew on me, it withered for him, and he eventually retreated back to California.

The relationship had its fatal flaws, of course, but my twenty-three-year-old self sees none of those, and that night I cling to the years of broken plans we had made.

I am inconsolable, and the next morning I drag myself to see the woman who has been teaching me about plants and homeopathy and how bodies can heal. I came to her when I first arrived in Mexico, ill and bedraggled from working too hard in college and graduate school. I had not been healthy for a long time, and she helped me regain my footing over the course of the year. With this setback, I need her more than ever.

She writes me a list of what I need to do. Eat almonds. Drink smoothies. Sleep. Be kind to yourself.

In those rare moments when I am able to pick myself up off the cool Mexican tiles, I find myself scanning flights to far-off lands. *Where do I want to go?* I think. And that is the thought that makes me happy.

Soon I am on a long plane ride to South Africa with Lara, a dear friend. It was a sudden, perhaps absurd, decision, one that lacked any planning at all save a phone call to guarantee we actually booked ourselves on the same flight. Since leaving Stanford the year before, we had thrown around the idea of traveling to Africa together several times but never formalized it so much as to actually open a guidebook or look at a calendar. She has just ended a relationship of her own, though, and convinces me the timing is perfect. We buy tickets and leave a few days later. "It's just what you need," she says.

And she is right.

We spend a month driving along the garden route, a picturesque coastline that reminds me of both the Caribbean and Nantucket—places I have only heard described and have never actually set foot on—and in that month we live a life of pure excess. Having scones with clotted cream at every single meal and staying up until all hours of the night, developing theories about life and how love can thrive in our lives.

Mostly, though, the energy Lara brings with her, and the energy of the country we are in, encourage newness. And so I do things that I believed I could never do. I skydive one day, the instructor marveling that he has never jumped with anyone who does not scream.

We call the national parks, ask for a safari recommendation, and end up at a lovely but down-at-the-heel establishment, where we see more animals before breakfast than we have in our entire lives. And then we ask for more.

On our homegrown safari drives, the eleven-year-old son of the proprietor proves the main font of information for our endless questions about the workings of the species we see: "Do all zebras have stripes?" "Is the rhino really the fastest?" "Who would win in a fight between a rhino and a lion?" "Who'd win between a tiger and a leopard?" "What about if there was an elephant there too?"

We are children in a candy store of wonder at Africa. This boy has no idea where he has the luck to live, we think. The trip is a pilgrimage and will remain one of the best trips of my life—because it almost didn't happen, because of all that would later come to pass in Africa, and because of Lara.

We had met the first day of our freshman year at Stanford University, where we lived across the hall from each other, and she immediately intimidated me with her designer clothes from Boston, a worldly story of being born in Egypt and growing up in Saudi Arabia, and a brand of confidence I had rarely seen. She didn't like me either in the beginning, and her singular memory of me in those first few months was of me running off to teach Sunday school and attend Christian retreats. Could she really ever be close to someone who was *so very* Christian? she thought.

But we did become friends, and our group of girls spent the college years building a strong and lasting bond. Lara and I studied together in Italy for six months, and over the years we shared in most of the things that make you grow up when you are twenty and learning it all. But even so, when the rest of our friends heard we were traveling together to South Africa, they had cautioned her, "Are you sure you can handle Claire *alone* right now?"

My sadness was a bit glaring, I suppose.

On our last day on the Western Cape, we do one of the things that a guidebook we bought in South Africa recommended. Joining many others, we take a crowded ferry to Robben Island, where one of the most symbolic prison complexes under apartheid opened its doors as a museum in 1995. Amazingly, the tours at Robben Island are given by the political prisoners who spent years of their lives confined in these suffocating rooms.

We see the toilets, the mess hall, the dog cages, and the garden, where men dug things for no reason at all eight hours a day and where Nelson Mandela hid his famous manuscript in the dirt. Throughout the afternoon everyone keeps pushing the question of our guide's own story—phrasing new questions that will encourage him to reveal anything at all. How was it a decade ago in this room when you were here? What was the food like, in your opinion? What was *your* experience?

And finally, toward the end of the afternoon, he leads us into a long dormitory room where some forty men slept on bunk beds. The beds are pushed against the back of the room now, and while a few tourists sit on the worn mattresses, the rest of us gather on the benches that have been nailed into the walls. He looks at us, smiling, and begins to tell us his story.

For the first time that day, the acoustics are good.

He was fifteen, or fourteen, or some age at which men should be worried about the aftershave they should buy or the girl they want to impress. Instead, he was living in the midst of political misery and the emerging dissidence that sought a way out. This landed him in jail, imprisoned for the rest of his foreseeable days. He was sixteen then and saw no way out. Although the details of his story are hazy, the outline is clear: dissidence for good cause, questionable means, unjust incarceration.

When he finishes his story, there is shuffling and a few coughs, and I look around the room at the tourists alongside me, leaning against the concrete walls. A teenage boy peers over the ledge to see the garden beyond.

Finally, an African American woman from the United States asks him, "How do you"—and by *you* she reiterates *you South Africans*— "forgive? How can you possibly forgive what happened here?"

He looks at her thoughtfully and nods his head. He hears that question often, this suggests. It is a question many are confused by, but there is no bewilderment in his voice. For him it is simple.

He says, "For us to pursue revenge would destroy us."

On the ferry back to Cape Town that day, everyone is jostling for pictures and glimpses of Robben Island from afar. I feel a bit happy to escape, and the relief translates into last shots of the island's penguins, mixed with silence. Lara and I watch a man sitting toward the back of the boat, his demeanor the only thing that appears to distinguish him from the tourists around him.

Looking at him—and determining he must be a guide—Lara says, "He's not turning back." I think about what she has said and wonder why the man doesn't look at the island as he floats away. Because he will see it in the morning? Because he will see it every day? Because it's in his dreams?

That night, our last in Africa, the man clouds our minds, and we talk about the ways that individuals can overcome such atrocities. The sheer enormity of the healing that has taken place is incredible, and I marvel that two decades ago the man in that cell could never have dreamed he would one day be called on to lead tourists from all corners of the globe through what was once his brutal reality.

I think about this, about forgiveness, about God, and about how we learn to accept the new changes in our lives.

And I see new dreams.

SAMMY

CHAPTER 3

My mother has still not returned, and soon our neighbors start making food for us. It feels good to see that people are there who care.

My brother and I know we have to learn how to live alone, even though I am barely ten years old, and more importantly, we know we need money to do so. First, we start selling some stuff in the house to make a few shillings. Then I come up with the idea to start a water project. I take water from the neighbors' water tap and put it in plastic bags, which I seal shut with fire. I then sell the packages of water at the school for a shilling. It is a good day when I sell five or sometimes ten, and we can buy a doughnut for my little sister, and Muriithi and I can share another one. There are times, though, we can only buy the one doughnut for Bethi, who is now five. On the worst days there is nothing even for her.

Then one day we get kicked out of our house, and all our belongings disappear.

Luckily, we run into one of my mother's new friends, one of the well-dressed ones, Mary. When she sees us, she gives us each fifty shillings and then tells us not to tell our mother. But we say we don't know where our mother is anyway, and we ask if she does. We tell her about our mother's new job in Nairobi and how she said she would come home to us on Wednesdays. Mary looks worried. She takes us to her home and calls our extended family.

When Mary tells them what we have told her, they say she should bring us to a family gathering in Nanyuki, the city in Kenya where my father's older brother lives, where the whole family is getting together for an event. When we arrive, Mary begins talking to the adults, telling them what has happened and asking someone to take us. But no one wants to. There are three of us, after all, and we are not in great shape. My sister is malnourished and doesn't walk well, and my brother has other problems. Two days later, though, my aunt Lydia Njeri agrees to take us in. She sends my sister to live with another aunt in Nairobi, and she takes my brother and me with her to Nyeri, a place far away where the people speak only Kikuyu.

Even though I was born of the Kikuyu tribe, I haven't had much practice in the language, and that is just one of the things about this place that surprises me. We immediately go from the white Nakuru dirt to the red dirt of Nyeri, and I smile in wonder at the green, green, green. There are trees and farms everywhere.

The house we are taken to is small and wooden and has two bedrooms and a living room. There is a kitchen outside and a smelly pit toilet where four cows walk in and out. The yard in front has banana trees, flowers, and a grassy area with a sugarcane plantation.

Many people are living there already—my aunt and her husband, my aunt's daughter, two other cousins, and four other kids. And there is even a new little boy, Xavier, for me to be a big brother to.

Most interesting of all, the house is near a beautiful place I have never heard of—a big mansion of a house called Imani Children's Home. Sometimes as I walk along the road to my new school, I look at that place and wonder what happens inside.

Life at my aunt's home is hard. There are many people living in the small space and too many mouths to feed. To help, my aunt decides to ask Imani Children's Home if we can come and eat lunch there during school days. The orphanage agrees, but even after a few months of that I can see my aunt is still having money troubles. She begins to ask us if the kind ladies at Imani have ever invited us to stay the night. It would be good for us, she says, to sleep on beds and have food every day, and I begin to think Imani must be a kind of paradise. A heaven, I think, where kids eat all the time and have free, clean clothes and no one ever gets a beating.

And then it happens.

One day at Imani, while I'm eating lunch as usual, the secretary calls me outside, where I find my brother waiting as well. I worry we have done something wrong, and I whisper to him, "Did you do something bad? Are you in trouble? Am I in trouble?"

The secretary, wearing a red dress and elegant high heels, says kindly, "How are we doing?" She asks me about my clothes.

"This is the only shirt I have for school," I say.

And then she asks us, "How would you like to live in a big house?"

"What big house—your house?" I ask, confused, because I have seen her family's house from the road when I walk to school.

"No, Sammy, you are not going to live in my house. Tomorrow you and Muriithi are going to come to Imani." I think this is a funny joke and start giggling. But she is serious. "Tomorrow you will have to bring all your clothes and everything you have with you when you come to school. After school, you will come here to Imani to live."

As soon as she says those words, I cannot express my happiness. It feels like the biggest wall in the world has just been taken down. It is like a door that has finally been opened with just one tiny push. And I think for a small moment that maybe if I am this happy, it will help me forgive my mother for what she has done.

I go back inside to eat my food, and I have a huge grin on my face.

People ask, "What happened? Why are you so happy?" And I tell them I have been invited to join Imani Children's Home. Some of the students are not pleased because they have not received their own invitations, but in that moment I don't think about that, because I am happy beyond control.

My brother is excited too, but he is also a little worried. At nearly fourteen, a couple years older than me, he still has health problems, and he worries what will happen when he lives in the big mansion house with all the other kids and what they'll say about him.

As I walk home, I am jumping with excitement, taking rocks and throwing them on the ground, watching for the little bumps as I might when I skip pebbles on water.

When I reach my aunt's, she has just gotten off work, and my uncle is also there. Joy fills my heart when I realize I will not have to face my uncle and his beatings anymore. In that moment, I know that I will never again fear going home at night. (Even today I remember that feeling.) As I look at my aunt, though, my heart sinks down inside me. It is sad to imagine having to leave the woman who has taken care of us. Even though she had many other kids in the house, she took in two more. All I want to do is give her a big hug and tell her, "Thank you."

That day my uncle and I walk in the field, and he calls me to his side. He tells me, "Sammy, I believe in you. I know I might have acted in strange ways, beating you and getting angry, but I do believe in you. When you go to Imani, I want you to be the best that you can be. One day I want to see you walking in step with the great

Reverend Mathu, the founder of the orphanage." He smiles. "No matter what, I want him to like you, and I want you to be a good kid. I know you will be."

He is my uncle, so I take his advice and keep it in my heart.

Later that night I ask my aunt, "How are we going to bring our clothes tomorrow to Imani?" So she gives us two store plastic bags, even though plastic bags are very valuable. One is for Muriithi and one is for me. I take my one pair of shorts and the other two shirts I have and put them in the bag. I then take my other little boyish things—the stick and grass toys I made in the field—and put them inside as well. That small bag is not very full.

This is when I feel it in my heart that I am not going to come back.

When I go to bed that night on the couch, I know that a chapter of my life is closing and another one is about to start.

The next morning is a different kind of morning. I can feel it. It is a Wednesday, and all good things that have happened to me in life have happened on a Wednesday.

The birds wake me, chirping, and the sound feels so sweet. The sun outside is just showing its light and shining golden on the fields, and I think that everything is more beautiful than it has been in a very long time. When I go outside to wash my face, I don't use the water from the well like I normally do, but I use the morning dew I find on the ground. I suppose I know this day is different from any other.

I go back into the house and pick up my school shirt and my school shorts and put them on. Then I realize that my brother has already gone to school and I am the only one still in the house. I drink my Kenyan tea and put the Blue Band margarine on my bread. It tastes delicious, and I eat it slowly.

As I walk to school, I think about the fact that it is the last day I will be walking this road, so I look at all the details as I go along. I walk carefully, and only after I finally arrive do I realize how late I am.

I am very late when I finally arrive at school, and the headmaster gives me two beatings with a cane and tells me to clean around the school.

But I am still happy.

When I look back now, I know that day was really not all that special. Instead, it was just a day like any other day. But that was not how it felt. Sometimes people wait for the best things in their lives, and they are surprised when they happen on a normal day. That normal day was one of the best days of my life.

At lunchtime, I go to Imani to eat as I normally do. As I eat the delicious ugali we always have on Wednesday—a thick, hard gruel of maize meal, milk, and water that you eat with a spoon—the secretary comes in and asks if I am ready.

I remember something I read in a book once and decide to use it now. I look up with a smile and say, "I am as ready as I will ever be!" After I say it and she looks at me funny, I realize it doesn't sound good in Swahili, and I remind myself not to say it again unless I am speaking English.

She tells me that as soon as school is finished, I am to come straight to Imani. And so when school gets out, I walk quickly to the orphanage gates and am directed to the matron's office. When I enter, she greets me cheerily.

"How are you doing?" she booms with her loud, happy voice.

I tell her I am fine, and she asks if I am ready.

Just as I am about to once again use my new line—"Ready as I will ever be!"—I stop myself. I am not going to say that again in Swahili, I remember.

"Yes," I tell her simply. "I am very ready."

So she starts to tell me about Imani. Even though I have been eating lunch here for a while, I don't know as much about the place as I think. She tells me about how Imani started when Reverend Mathu, the man my uncle mentioned, joined with some people from the United States to build a big, beautiful mansion of a building for children in the community who needed a place to live. Then she tells me the rules of the orphanage as she takes me up to the room I will be sharing with my roommates.

As soon as she is done showing me around, I start meeting new people and making friends. Although I have met many of the kids before, they have never been my friends, because there is a separation between those who eat in the orphanage at lunch and those who live there all the time. That division, I come to see, has to do with protection. I soon learn that the kids who live in the orphanage don't make lots of friends with kids who live outside it, because they are trying to guard themselves from being made fun of and, at the same time, from being the objects of jealousy.

I am still introducing myself to the boarders when it comes time for tea at 4:00 p.m. I didn't know the students took tea at the orphanage, and I am excited. Three meals and tea!

Two hours later it is the moment I have been waiting for—dinner! We go down to the wooden kitchen to eat my favorite ugali maize meal for the second time that day. This time I am given a cup, a plate, and a spoon and told to keep them for myself. We say grace and then start lining up to be served the food. As I get closer to the front of the line, I am shocked by the size of the pots holding the ugali and beans. I give the servers my plate and they put a huge piece of ugali on it, and then on the side they put a mountain of beans.

I sit down and eat hungrily as people laugh and smile around me. Then I notice that a few people are saving parts of their ugali.

I wonder why they are doing that, remembering that the rules the manager gave me say we cannot save food. But I realize they are secretly saving it in their shirts so they can eat it with breakfast in the morning because, like me, they like it so much. I take note of that.

After dinner, we go back to our rooms, and I am told it is study time. I take my books and go to the study hall, where everyone sits around reading and doing homework. I am amazed that I will actually have people to help me—it is just one more great thing about this place. During study hall, the matron calls on me to come downstairs, where she gives me a piece of soap, a towel, and a new toothbrush. There are no clothes to sleep in, but what I already have is more than enough. At 10:30 p.m., we go to sleep.

The next morning I am woken up at 5:00 to take a cold shower in a bucket, as I have done all my life. I then dress quickly in my uniform of khaki shorts and checkered green and white shirt. The clothes are hand-me-downs and very thin, and I don't have any socks. The funniest part of all is my shoes, which people come to call *laughing shoes* because the front part opens like a mouth. People soon start teasing me by saying, "Hey, Sammy, you're still smiling and so are your shoes!"

At 6:00 a.m. we go for breakfast down at the little wood cabin. The servers give us big plastic mugs of uji, a maize meal like ugali that is mixed with a lot of milk, water, and sugar. I love it, and I love it even more when they give me seconds.

When I walk back to the dorms, I see people brushing their teeth, so I decide I better do what they are doing. I take out my new toothbrush and squeeze out toothpaste like I see others around me doing. Everything is new.

After morning class, I come back to Imani for lunch and then return to school for the afternoon. When school ends, I walk back through the churchyard and the gardens and start doing my duties, which include washing my clothes. Since I only have one pair of shorts and one shirt for school, I have to be careful to wash them quickly in the afternoon so they can dry. I will wait until the weekend to wash my sweater.

I get used to my routine, and each day passes quickly until the time at night when the matrons lock us inside our dormitory rooms to sleep.

I soon see that Imani is a strict place. The girls are on one side and the boys are on the other. You cannot go to the other side without getting in a lot of trouble, and the matrons are strict with kids who break rules.

The first time I see someone get in trouble, it is my friend Ephantus, who is a few years younger than me. He is always trying to bend the rules, and apparently he had gotten into the habit of trying to make things easy for himself when it came to clothes washing. He decided that things would be much faster if he could take a shower and wash his clothes at the same time! Someone told on him, though, because one day the matron secretly watched as he did just that. She got angry and punished him severely. *Wow!* I thought. *This lady is not joking!* That was the first time I realized how strict the two matrons who look after us can really be.

Weekends are a bit more relaxed for everyone. They begin on Friday night with worship, where we kids sing, dance, and pray together. Worship is run by the older students, and neither the two matrons nor the manager, who live with us, usually attend. It is a really unique time and something everyone loves, as it gives us the chance to sing our hearts out to the Lord—to scream, to cry, to get it all out. For hours we jump up and down, singing every song we know. Then we watch as our peers present their own songs, Bible verses, and speeches. It is an amazing time I come to look forward to each week.

On Saturdays we have breakfast around 7:00 a.m., and then afterward we clean the floors and do our duties. After that, the majority of us wash all our clothes—including the sweaters we haven't been able to wash during the week because they won't dry fast enough. We also clean our shoes. Kenyans love their shoes, and the few kids with sports shoes spend forever washing them carefully. We diligently wipe down our black school shoes.

During the day the high school kids like my brother study. We primary kids study as well, or at least we call it that. In reality, we just play the whole day. In the afternoon we watch the high school students play in their football games, then we eat dinner, shower, and go to bed.

On Sundays it is the same kind of relaxed life, and we have a special breakfast everyone looks forward to of bread, margarine, and jam alongside boiled eggs. After breakfast, we go to church and Sunday school. And then it is more football, studying, and homework. Sunday lunch—rice and beans—is a huge favorite, and it is delicious. At 4:00 we have tea and play card games and checkers or volleyball. After dinner, we "study" some more and then get ready for school the next day.

As the days pass, I come to see that the kids at Imani really are their own kind of family. To get inside their circle, you have to gain their trust. Although I know many of them because I went to school with them before coming to live at Imani, I am still an outsider. I also see how important the older girls—the "big sisters"—are to taking care of all the little kids. Later on I hear international volunteers ask how it is possible that nearly two hundred students have only three adults to take care of them full-time. Those big sisters are the reason.

It is interesting to me to see how the concept of family plays out at Imani. Even though people might not have a blood family, they take whatever is available and make a family for themselves.

Throughout the years I will see this become true for me again and again.

One of the different things about life at the orphanage is that Imani hosts some international visitors, and this is a whole new world for me. Many of these volunteers come from churches far away, stay for two or three days, and then leave forever.

Dr. Eve, though, is a woman who always comes back.

Dr. Eve has been around Imani since it started, so even when I was only eating lunch at Imani and not yet living here, I had heard of her from other kids and had even seen her from time to time. I don't know her personally, though, and all I know about her comes from the stories I have heard. She is a reverend in the United States, the students say, and she is on the board of directors for Imani because she has helped the orphanage and Reverend Mathu so much. Everyone always talks about her, and I am intrigued.

When she comes back to Kenya for the first time since I started living at Imani, I go directly up to her and say, "Hello!"

She booms, "Hello!" right back and asks who I am.

This is the first time we have ever talked, and what interests me most is that she isn't like other visitors to Imani. She doesn't say, "Photos!" and then "Bye!" She actually talks to me. Even though I am just a kid, we have a real conversation, and it feels really good.

This is when I first begin to understand some of the many problems that come when people from the United States visit us in Kenya. The typical visitor at Imani shows up without knowing anyone, volunteers a few hours, takes pictures, and then leaves. All without finding out who lives in the orphanage and who we really are as people. It is terrible for us kids, and it makes us feel mad and hurt all at the same time.

Then, for the first time, the orphanage has volunteers from overseas stay at the home for longer than a few days. Two married volunteers come from a big place with few people called Alaska to stay for a whole year. Mr. and Mrs. Thomas are younger than our two matrons, and they end up becoming two of the best people I ever meet. Like every other kid who lived at Imani when Mr. and Mrs. Thomas lived there, I will keep them in my heart forever. For many of us, knowing them helped us understand there were people similar to us living all over the world.

One of the great things Mr. and Mrs. Thomas start is Saturday games, which will continue for years after they leave. On Saturday afternoons they set out board games in the dining hall for us to play with. I have not seen many games before, and one day they teach a group of six or seven of us to play a game called Monopoly. I can't believe my excitement, as it is so fast-paced and fun. After we are done playing that day, for the whole next week all I can think is, *I can't wait for Saturday. I'm going to go to school so that the days are over quickly and I can get to play Monopoly again.* The whole week I hold my breath as I wait to play again.

Mr. Thomas also introduces me to card tricks. One day I am going to dinner and see a group of boys gathered around Mr. Thomas. When I walk up, he is doing a card trick. I have never seen anything like it. *Whoa,* I think. *How does he do that?* I am mesmerized and cannot take my eyes off the cards. That night I decide once and for all, "Mr. Thomas is a magician." I had heard about magicians on TV for the first time earlier that year, and I can't wait to ask Mr. Thomas to show me how to do the trick. He does, and for years after I do card tricks when visitors come.

One day in seventh grade I am doing homework and come across a long division problem. It is something I should have learned in fifth grade, but fourth, fifth, and sixth grades were bad years for me. I lived alone with my brother, then with my aunt and her mean husband, and along the way I was never eating enough or going to school regularly, and I was always getting beaten. It affected me, I know, and kept me from concentrating in school and caring about my studies.

I have absolutely no idea how to do the problem, but I am embarrassed, so I tell my friend Njoki that someone else asked me to help them with the problem, but I'm not certain how to teach them—could she show me how I can best help them? I am embarrassed to know nothing, but because I have skipped so much school, there are a lot of holes in my education.

Slowly, with the help of the good food at Imani and the support of friends, I start getting better. I keep improving, and in the second term, I find myself in the middle of the pack of students. By the third term, I am placed number three in the whole class of seventh graders. I am proud that I have improved, little by little.

Even though some international volunteers later aren't so sure, I always think that Imani does a good job taking care of our health. When we get sick, they take us to the clinic, and the matrons make us shower every single day. Most importantly, we look out for each other. The high school boys, if they suspect someone has not been showering for a while, even take that person and shower him themselves! They pick him up and carry him to the bathing area, bring the water, and then scrub him and pour water on him.

The visitors also help. One time a doctor comes to talk about teeth brushing. She tells us how one day she dropped her toothbrush in the toilet room, but she didn't throw it out. Instead, she boiled it. We think that is gross, but then she makes herself clear. If the toothbrush drops on the floor of the toilet, you can boil it and use it again. If it drops inside the toilet, do not use it again.

She tells us to boil all our toothbrushes every two weeks. We do not do that, though.

Food at the orphanage is good, and it is very important. It can make two people the best of friends or the worst of enemies. If you mess with someone's food, there are going to be problems. But if you help someone protect their food or get them more, you are going to be best friends.

We eat together as a family in the small wooden dining halls. (This is before we get even more students and move to the new, large dining hall.) Because there are so many people, the cooks make the food in large pots for everyone.

We have beans almost every day. No matter what, we eat beans. Githeri is a mixture of beans and maize, and we eat that at all our meals on Mondays, Tuesdays, and Fridays. On Wednesdays we mix my favorite ugali with bean stew. On Thursdays we have rice with beans, everybody's favorite. Sundays are the best days, when we have rice and beans for lunch and then ugali for dinner. Just like I saw other students do that first day, I start to save my ugali when we have it, then take it to bed and eat it in the morning for breakfast.

At Imani, I come to love reading books. Since there isn't much to do except for school and chores, reading becomes one of my favorite hobbies, and I am amazed that Imani has its own library. Most of the books have been donated by Christian missionaries and overseas churches, and there are a lot of Christian books. There is one series I love—the Magic Tree House books. I earn a gift when I fill three library cards with books I check out, and I am really happy.

Aside from reading, I also love participating in church programs, like Brigades, which is similar to Boy Scouts but is sponsored by the Presbyterian Church. Like the church youth group, it occupies my time and helps me stay out of trouble. It helps me start to become a young leader and opens up new opportunities for me. When I do eventually join the youth group, I am recognized because I am actively involved in Brigades.

As time passes, I reach the eighth grade. It has been a year since I joined Imani as a boarder, and time has gone quickly. Eighth grade is a big year for me, and for all Kenyans, since it is the year we have to take a huge national test called the KCPE, which will determine if we can continue on to secondary school. If you fail the KCPE, no high school invites you to join. I study for months and pray hard.

It is at this time that a new manager joins Imani Children's Home. Her name is Eunice, and she is a great Christian woman who loves God with her whole heart. Since she has been very active in the Presbyterian Church of East Africa (PCEA), most people at Giakombe parish—the parish that Imani Children's Home and the orphanage church are part of—already know her. One month into her time at Imani, she comes up to me and says, "Sammy, you're one person who has really great potential. Make sure you study, and study hard. Get good grades." She says this as though she really believes in me and believes I will score well on my important KCPE exams.

It is also during this time that I get to know Reverend Mathu, or Guka. Guka, which means "grandfather" in Kikuyu, is the man my uncle once told me he hoped I would know. He is the reverend who started Imani Children's Home, and he has been at Giakombe parish for a long, long time. He is good friends with the treasurer of Imani, whom we call Cucu ("grandmother" in Kikuyu)—a very strict, very loving woman who always gives us words of caution and advice.

Soon the year with Mr. and Mrs. Thomas comes to a close, and our second missionary couple moves in. Mr. and Mrs. Thomas have set a high bar, and Paul and Stephanie try as much as possible to live up to what they have accomplished. They both teach in the local school. Paul, who is studying to become a pastor, teaches Christian religious education, and Stephanie teaches English.

Dr. Eve, Mr. and Mrs. Thomas, and Paul and Stephanie all teach me that mzungus, or white people, don't always leave after just a few hours and a few hundred pictures. But it will be two other mzungus who teach me that sometimes mzungus stay in your life forever.

CLAIRE

CHAPTER 4

One month after our trip across South Africa ends, I am in an internet café in China, begging Lara to travel with me around the world for a year.

"For *real* this time," I write. "A *year*."

Up late at night in San Francisco, she responds within minutes. "I'm in. Just promise me we will *really* plan things this time."

In the end, any planning we do will consist of me drawing a map of the world on a napkin and dotting regions of the globe we'd like to visit.

To begin the year right, Lara shaves her head.

It is a month before we leave, and we are watching *Saturday Night Live* with our friend Amalia in San Francisco, where I am visiting friends and family before setting off on the trip. A famous actress is guest starring, looking great with her new short haircut for her latest terrorist movie.

Lara, out of the blue, says, "I might want to shave my head."

Amalia and I, distracted, barely acknowledge her. She can't be serious, of course.

But then Lara says it again. "Yeah, I mean, I've thought about it."

With minimal prodding from two friends who are amazed at the idea of knowing someone who would actually willingly shave her head, we drive to Walgreens to buy the clippers.

Within an hour, it is done, we have emailed the photos to everyone we know, and we are one step closer to leaving.

We begin the trip with a two-week cruise from Miami to Spain, where I'll run my first marathon. I finish my training on the cruise ship, pounding out miles on the tiny track on the upper deck—fourteen laps equals a mile—and filling my body with richer food than we will see for months. After Madrid, we head south to Granada and then to Morocco, where we spend a night in the desert, nearly tripping over tiny kittens drinking milk from teacups on the sand dunes.

Although we spend some days on the road truly traveling—rising early for a bus or plane—the majority of our days start late, in a cheap hotel or hostel somewhere with a long breakfast and lots of tea. We spend a good chunk of every day working at our freelance jobs, earning enough to offset the expenses of the trip, and then typically take a long walk around where we are that day or week, in search of a cute place for lunch or dinner. Tourist attractions are not our goal—to preserve your sanity you can't spend a year in museums, we decide—and we instead focus on attempting to live our strange lives in a new place from week to week.

A few months into our year on the road, we stay for a month on the beach in southern India, where the daily monsoons mirror my mood. I stay up nights, making lists of all that I love about my life and wondering why I still feel so blue about lost love. Shouldn't travel be curing me?

One day while in Goa, India, I have the best day.

It doesn't start that way, but rather it starts as one of those hard days, something we all have, when things are going on in life and we feel sad about them. But on the trip, when we have them, Lara and I like to use a phrase of our friend Mari, and we look at each other and say, "But you can't have a bad day—because you're *living the dream!*"

So on the best day—perhaps calling a bad day *the best day* helps to make it so—I go out for a run on the beach, because running has been one thing that I have learned in the last year is making me a better me. I used to hate running something fierce, but now it is changing me. And it is on the run that something happens that makes that best day actually, truly, one of the best days I've had in a long, long time.

I am running, and I come across all these ferocious-looking, probably rabid dogs. And I get kind of scared but then tell myself that there are really only three, that they even look mildly playful, and that I can run into the ocean and outswim them with my paltry arm muscles if they try to viciously attack me. So I keep running. This may not seem like a big deal, but it is, because I used to be terrified of dogs, and only in the past couple years, with the help of a tiny dog in Mexico, have I been able to slowly start to like them a bit.

So after I safely pass the dogs, I realize all of a sudden that there is a little one running behind me. I get scared because it looks like he's trying to bite my calf, but I breathe deeply and keep running. And he just hangs in there. The dog and I run up and down the beach together for a long, long time, and it is weirdly wonderful.

A few times I start to worry that the dog is getting worn out because he is so far behind, so I clap my hands and say encouraging things like, "Come on now, buddy!" And he comes running like a crazy man really fast, and I realize that he wasn't tired at all, he just thought I was slow and was giving me a head start so it didn't get boring for him. (Kind of like skiing with parents or a boyfriend, I think.)

At some point, I start to feel really, really warm feelings for the dog I can't control, and I remember that on 1950s television shows and Disney family movies, sometimes people throw sticks and dogs catch them. So I go out and find a dead tree near the beach and get a stick that I think looks about right. We start playing this game, fetch, which is perhaps the most out-of-body experience I've ever had, given what I feel for dogs.

He's not that good at it and never manages to actually bring the stick back, but instead he just sits there with it in his mouth, waiting for me to come get it. And so we move down the beach like that, and I keep thinking about what compelled me to go find the stick in the first place, because playing with dogs (especially with sticks) is not the kind of thing I do.

And then, because it is southern India in summertime, the monsoon starts. The rain gets really, really, really hard and hurts my eyelids, and I can't see more than fifteen feet around me. But I don't want to go in, because it feels like a cleansing that I need badly, so I stand there on the beach just feeling the rain.

I look down and realize that the dog is huddled up against me to protect himself from the rain, and it feels like I am helping the dog by just being there and that he needs me, and in that moment I feel more lucky than I've been in a long while.

After about fifteen minutes of me just standing there, looking at the dog hiding behind my legs and being in the rain, it starts to let up and the sky fills with insane white light. It feels like the apocalypse in a really good way and is pretty amazing. I keep looking for a rainbow but there isn't one, though I think maybe if you *think* there is a rainbow, even if you can't see it, it's the same thing. Then the rain stops and the sand is completely clean and our footprints are all gone, and it's like the beach is being born.

Even though my run is over, the dog and I do this really weird thing and start running some *just for fun*. And it makes me remember why I have decided that, in a small way, I may actually like dogs. And here is why: they are happy little guys, they make you exercise and go outside, and they just radiate love.

When I come back from the run, I say to Lara, "I ran with a dog!"

"But you hate dogs!" she says. "And you hate running! Or you used to, at least."

"I know!" I say triumphantly.

And then I tell her the whole story of what happened, with the fetch and the dog and the warm feelings and all, and I even say that Jesus might have been coming down when the light got all weird.

To which she says, without looking up from her work, "I'm sure it was him, Claire," which is kind of a sarcastic comment because it's unclear what Lara thinks about Jesus.

Another month we visit our college friend Sue, who is on vacation with her family in a villa in Tuscany and has generously invited us to come stay for a week. The villa is filled with a handful of New England families, and for some of the adults it is the longest vacation they have had in thirty years. One couple is celebrating having their children's college educations finally mostly paid for.

"This is really our reward," the environmental lawyer says as he jumps into the pool.

One night there is a potluck dinner on the veranda overlooking the countryside—there is no veranda at the villa that does not overlook such a view—and we drink wine and eat fresh pasta for hours.

At one point in the night, the discussion heatedly turns toward doing good and international goodwill. No one knows that the study of this fine art is what fuels me, and I listen silently as the discussion unfolds. One of the men, who thinks I have not understood, turns to me and says simply, "They're talking about charity."

One of the couples with two children already grown will be leaving the villa at the end of the week to travel to Africa to adopt two children. But how can they get more L.L. Bean gear for the kids at the orphanage onto the plane? the husband wonders. The taxes can be so high when you go in those kinds of countries, another woman says. There is a whole industry built around trying to get this kind of stuff figured out, she adds.

Another woman explains her plan to spend seventy dollars a year to send an African child to make bread in Italy. The best part, she says, is that they can one day go visit the bread-making child, on the very same trip where she'll also visit a place she volunteered at thirty years ago.

"Why does he have to go to Italy to learn to make bread?" her twenty-something son asks from the other end of the table.

The conversation soon derails into the merits of sending a check overseas versus going there in person to volunteer, and I am amazed that the same conversation can happen everywhere.

We spend several weeks hiking to Everest Base Camp, and our guide, Lal, is the smelliest man I have ever met. But he is quiet and kind and struts ahead of us for the two weeks, drawing arrows in the dirt that tell us where to go when we can't see him. In a tiny teahouse in the high Himalayas, we meet a Dutch woman we take to be someone like us—a person who doesn't belong on a mountain much bigger than she is.

But she is not that at all, it turns out, and she tells us she summited Mount Everest in 1999, and then her stories start tumbling out. She tells us of the inexperienced climbers she has seen tumble to their deaths and says it is a pity that people no longer climb just for the love of the mountain. Last year she met a blind Dutch man making the climb, and days before he ended up dying on the mountain she asked him, "Why are you really doing this?"

Everyone goes now, she says. Just to say they have. "What to do?" she says, shrugging her shoulders, swearing this will be her last climb.

In the end, the woman confesses that she did her Everest climb while going through a divorce.

"Typical life reinvention," Lara says the next day as we hike away. She means it in a good way, but I'm not sure the Dutch woman and I are so different. Isn't that what I am doing, after all?

Then Lara tells me the story about her brother and his trek in the Himalayas ten years before. He had a guide, she says, who told him simply, "Look when look, walk when walk."

Lara has always done that better than I can, I think.

In Thailand, we stay on a beautiful island called Ko Lanta, where the two headwaiters at the lodge we stay at met and married after he saved her from the tsunami two years before.

I spend days writing a letter that will be read in a courtroom in San Francisco, where a judge will decide if my father will go to prison or if his appeal will save him. My father is a journalist, and he has exposed one of the most famous sports stars in America for steroid use. The year before, the government subpoenaed him for his sources, and when he told them that giving up his sources is against everything his profession stands for, they sentenced him to eighteen months in prison.

I have spent an inordinate amount of time on this letter, and I have two versions. This morning I must decide which to send. I remember a book I read once in Mexico about a woman who used the I Ching, opening it up at a random point to help her determine something important about her life, so I do the same thing with my Bible, the small Spanish version Lara and I bought on the Canary Islands. I open it up and land on Colossians 4:6: "Let your conversation be always full of grace."

I take this to mean to send the nicer of the two letters, the pleading one, the one that points no barbs at the injustice.

After sending it, I wander out to the beach to think and stand looking at all the garbage I had seen when running earlier that day. As I walk along, I see a shower curtain with the green fur of mold, a syringe, a Pond's acne gel tube. I wonder about how much more dramatic it would have been after the tsunami, when the remains of the lodge's spa would have been mixed in with the everyday garbage of always.

I am feeling tense and jittery and scour the resort's equipment shack for a plastic bag, because I think that picking up garbage will do wonders to calm me. The repetitive motion, the mindless movement—like when a high school boyfriend once broke up with me while counting change.

I can't find a bag of any kind, though, so I take a seat on the sand and go back to my Bible and the book of James. Just then a small boy of five or six walks onto the beach, dressed head to toe in a wet suit, cap, and snorkeling gear. He had been at the pool earlier that day, and I had watched him contemplate the dark, inky water. Now the boy and his mother walk to the surf, and he acts much as he did at the pool, except this time the thrill of approaching water makes him wild with excitement. I watch the boy scream with delight as each calmly approaching wave grazes his foot, and I put the Bible aside.

All is going well for the mother and the boy until suddenly he slips and falls down into the shallow but fast-moving water the wave has left. And I don't fully understand how, but all of a sudden he is tumbling head over heels in a kind of jumbled ball that I wouldn't have thought possible, given that nothing appears to have actually happened. But I scramble up because I am bored and because his things are flying about, and I start hopping awkwardly through the shallow waves in search of all he has lost. He is crying as his mother pulls him to his feet, and they both stumble to high ground.

"Is okay, ma'am!" his mother begins to shout, but I have nearly come upon his cap (neck flaps still attached) and am playing what I hope will be a short game of tag with it beneath each coming wave. When I get it, victorious and fairly breathless, I ask if there is anything else, and she makes a motion near her face: the tube from his snorkel is gone too.

The prospects look bleak, as I see nothing of the sort, and that item's particular construction lends it to the possibility of prompt sinking. I am agitated, though, and want to solve this, so I begin dancing about in the waves, hoping something will come to me. The mother sees it is hopeless, because she starts a long chain of "Is okay, ma'am," which she continues for far too long as I refuse to take in that the thing has really disappeared.

I am worried, you see, that the boy won't go back in, and that he'll always remember this early nasty experience with the ocean and not want to come back, and somehow it seems that finding the tube—showing that the ocean did not take it from him after all—will make it better.

As they start walking up the beach to the safety of the lodge, where a calm pool can host the young snorkeler, the mother keeps yelling, "Is okay, ma'am."

At some point I stop looking, because the tube is a hopeless cause (and has been since the beginning), and I go back to sitting on the beach, thinking about how hot it is, and the letter I have sent, and how wild with excitement the boy was before swimming, and then the fall and the crying and the lost things. And how even all the good equipment he had on could not totally protect him.

I tell myself that it *is* okay, that there's only so much we can do, and that our best is enough. And if we are healthy enough, and if we have the right types of support and some calm pools to be in before and after, we can regroup and then once again face the ocean. And maybe it will be better next time.

On the five-year anniversary of September 11, Lara and I find ourselves in a country that is learning well to forgive.

Arriving in the airport in Hanoi, Vietnam, late at night a few nights earlier, we learn we've missed the twenty-hour train south to Hoi An, where we've booked a hotel. We are annoyed and try to blame each other and start a self-pitying rant about home that always indicates that things have really gone downhill—we whine for cell phones, and knowing what time zone we're in, and Mexican food, and having enough clothes to dress appropriately for an occasion, and Jon Stewart, and getting our points across, and people who understand us.

Quite simply, it is a night when another logistical nightmare with people we can't communicate with might just put us over the edge. Luckily, though, Vietnam steps up. Specifically, two kind individuals at an airport information tourist booth look at us—the sad beings we must have appeared to be—and decide to make it all better. For half an hour, they ask us kind questions about home and present simple travel options from which we can proactively carve out the next few days of our lives as we wait for a bus, and they smile over and over. And, of course, they refuse all money.

And at that moment, Vietnam seems a genuinely lovely place to be.

Over the next couple days driving south on the bus, we talk a lot about how incredible those two individuals were to us just when we needed it, and what it said about this country that they could give us our best experience at getting things done overseas, even when the bus can't go more than thirty-five kilometers an hour because the roads our country helped destroy a generation ago have never been fixed. The farther south we get, the nicer everyone seems to be, and we feel amazed and happy—especially when nobody stops being nice when we say we're from the United States, which we had worried about because we feel pretty sad about some of the things our country did here.

And when it becomes September 11 and we stand in a shop with a tailor watching names of the deceased being read at Ground Zero, we begin to talk about how lucky this world would be if they could pull off this kind of miracle of forgiveness in the Middle East by the time our daughters are traveling there.

There are themes that come up on such an anniversary, five years after something very terrible, and we can name them. Here is one: forgiveness. Like most everything in life that is really worth something, forgiveness can be really hard. There is an easier kind of forgiveness that we see more often in our world, when the bad thing is reversed and you get what you want in the end: when your sister buys you a new cashmere sweater to replace the one she ruined, when the teacher decides at the last minute that you can do extra credit not to fail, or when the judge changes his mind and grants the appeal. And this mini-forgiveness does have merit, and it makes you think a lot, and learn, and grow.

But the harder kind, the kind of forgiveness that is most difficult to come by, is when whatever you lost is really gone—because the doctor just can't do any more, or because the towers really did fall, or because things just will never be the same. And it's the harder kind that is the most important to find.

I do a lot of thinking about forgiveness. There are many reasons for this, including the fact that I came out of the womb judgmental and cranky when people don't act the way I want them to, and the fact that I like to complain that things aren't fair (except when I'm getting the good stuff, and that happens because God likes me and because I deserve it, obviously).

Sometime last year I was reading a book that talked about forgiveness, and it had a line in it that got me upset. It made the assertion that the phrase everyone says, "I can forgive, but I can't forget," is actually not true, not by a million light-years. Instead, it said that in order to truly forgive, you actually do kind of have to forget. At least somewhat, because remembering the specifics of hurts is usually just a way to catalog how good you've become at forgiving, and how much you've overcome, and how much better you are than the evil force that did the bad things to you.

I was working through this thought in my mind during our trip to South Africa the year before, when we went to Robben Island, the prison where Nelson Mandela spent so much of his life.

I remember the day well, when the ex-prisoner who was our tour guide told our group about why he decided to forgive, and then the ferry ride back to Cape Town where Lara and I watched a man sitting toward the back of the boat whom we recognized as a guide. His shoes seemed different, his way of looking out at the water was different, and he was alone. And although none of these things individually would add up to him being an ex-prisoner and guide, with all of them together we knew that he was. And when Lara realized that he seemed to be the only person on the ferry not looking back at Robben Island, I thought it meant something.

In the year and a half since, I have tried to write about the experience and have sent Lara strange emails out of the blue to ask her if she has an answer yet. If she has figured out yet why he wasn't looking back.

In Vietnam, a year and a half later, we talk about that man. She says she still isn't sure why the man didn't turn his head to look at Robben Island, and neither am I. But I think that maybe it has to do with him trying to forget and trying to forgive a little more each day. As we talk about the man, and forgiveness, and September 11, and everything that happened that day, we say how much we miss the Africa we had started to see, and how we'd like to go back.

CLAIRE

CHAPTER 5

Kenya is our nineteenth country, and our last.

Along the way, we go to Lara's birthplace of Cairo and see a beautiful church built into the side of a mountain with a stench like nothing we have ever smelled. All the city's garbage workers live here—the Christians whose religion doesn't forbid them from working alongside the garbage-sorting hogs.

I lose my passport in China, only discovering that fact when the Mongolian border police kick us off a midnight train as we try to enter their country. We spend a pleasantly dull week in the Chinese border town, twiddling our thumbs as our mothers, on the other side of the globe, sit terrified at our predicament. We blog about it, which sets them off even further, and I find my mother in the comments section, writing in capital letters to the effect of: STOP BLOGGING. CALL ME.

We board the Trans-Siberian Railway in Siberia, bound for Moscow. The dust seeps in through every crack of the train, and I am miserable. Two days later we jump off and fly the rest of the way.

We come to Kenya to climb a mountain.

On Everest, altitude sickness had me shivering in a sleeping bag for a full day and night before Lara, holding my hand, forced me to stumble down several thousand feet to clearheadedness in what was surely the slowest day of hiking known to man. We hear, though, that one experience with the sickness doesn't predict another, so we look to climb again, this time in the heart of the Africa we missed.

A friend of Lara meets us in Nairobi for the climb and brings with her a recommendation from a family friend of an inexpensive guesthouse we can stay at near the base of the mountain. We gladly accept. The fact that an orphanage owns the guesthouse is immaterial; it is just a place to sleep.

We spend a few days in Nairobi first, getting to know the capital while we luxuriate in a lovely cottage in the suburb of Karen, named for one of my favorite authors—Karen Blixen of *Out of Africa* fame. We see the house she lived in and visit a giraffe sanctuary where the animals have a trick of eating out of tourists' mouths. We take a video and put it on our blog, which, in the year since we started it, has become more popular than we ever imagined. Many thousands are still reading about our hapless travels.

The morning we set out to make the journey to the guesthouse near the mountain, we take tea in the picturesque suburban garden while waiting for the ride the orphanage has kindly arranged. There is a series of loud honks at the gate, and we are surprised when a truckload of Kenyan teens pulls into the drive in a yellow van, telling us to get in back.

We do, and we try to make sense of it all and where we are going. I know almost nothing about what Imani Children's Home is and why it owns a guesthouse, and I am baffled as to why there are so many people in the van.

"Are they orphans?" I whisper to Lara as we reach the outskirts of Nairobi, jostling together on the bench seats in the cramped compartment. And then, "Why are they all *here*?" In the typical over-the-top hospitality that we would come to learn Imani is known for, a dozen teens had been sent on an eight-hour round trip to bring us to our night's lodging at the guesthouse on their property.

By the time we near the guesthouse outside of Nyeri, I am famished. Our lunch of biscuits (sweet cookies, as we know them in the United States; "bees-quits" as the Imani kids pronounce them) at a roadside gas station—although ideal for the nausea-inducing roads—did little to curb my appetite, and when the teens say we've been invited to a late lunch with the church elders who run the orphanage and guesthouse, we readily agree. We tumble out of the van and pass lush green gardens as we enter a small building that stands in a loose cluster near a large three-story orphanage, a church, and an imposing dining hall. Lunch has been laid out on a long table.

It is in the middle of the lunch that something changes. Maybe it is the little girl I glimpse weeding the orphanage gardens with a smile as wide as Oklahoma, or the bright yellow sun on the grassy lawns, or the milk tea and food in my belly. Or maybe it is the sign I didn't know I was looking for.

I ask to use the restroom and am taken to a simple, spotless room where an old mirror hangs over the sink. As I look in that mirror, I have a moment I have never had before or since, where I can feel something changing, and I ask God to let me see.

"If you have put this place in my road to change me," I say, looking at my scratched reflection, "please open my eyes so I can see."

After lunch, we go to meet the children, a few of whom have already shyly come up to us. When Lara rounds up a group of kids to play Duck, Duck, Goose, I ask to be let into the orphanage's small library. I had volunteered briefly in New Orleans with my friend Amalia after Hurricane Katrina and had spent an entire day in a community center trying to put order to their books. Here I think of doing the same thing. The library, for me, feels a safer way to connect with the kids. In Egypt, we had spent an hour at a children's home while in transit to somewhere else, and I had felt so uncomfortable—paranoid about giving the children attention, about hurting them, about seeming a white savior who was here today and gone tomorrow. I remember the strong sense that I shouldn't interact with them too much unless I could offer them more than simply leaving.

That day in Kenya, Lara doesn't overthink things like I do, and I hear happy shouts from the lawn. In the library, I am impressed by the number of books in the space and immediately set to work trying to organize things better. Slowly, small children, surprised the library is open on a weekday, start filtering in.

Although I love children, and these children are lovely, in the library I can't help but feel sad as I watch them, hating the idea that they are somehow pandering to me—the white visitor. Hating the idea that they try to be cute. Hating the idea that the small attention I am giving them this afternoon is so craved. Hating that I will soon leave.

At one point in the afternoon, a small, skinny boy comes in, watching me as I read to a group of little ones. We start talking, and I am amazed at how his English is far, far better than that of any of the other children I have met that day. When he tells me how much he likes our senator Obama, I am taken aback, and it intensifies my feeling that this boy, who doesn't look more than ten, must truly be special.

After we eat dinner with the children at the dining hall, we retreat to the orphanage's guesthouse. That night I tell Lara I am thinking about staying at the orphanage and not climbing Mount Kenya at all. Another idea starts to form in my head, one in which we come back here for a longer period of time. We have been traveling for nine months at that point, but we both feel that we somehow aren't done yet and have been wondering what could be next. I say some of these things to Lara, and she nods agreeably, nonchalantly open to such a big new thing.

When Lara and her friend Kelly leave for the climb, I decide to fast on the decision and tell myself I will read the whole Bible before eating again. This, I believe, will take three days. I am a fast reader and can skim some of the Old Testament, I figure. I have never fasted before.

The orphanage staff thinks it beyond strange that I want to stay alone in the guesthouse, but they allow me to do so. The house is not far from the orphanage, after all, and there are two night watchmen and a caretaker, so they agree.

I start fasting Friday night and spend most of Saturday reading the Bible and talking with John, the guesthouse's caretaker, who still remains one of the more hysterical characters I ever met in Kenya. We throw barbs back and forth all weekend as I hide from him the fact I'm not eating—unsure of how the concept of fasting goes over in a place of so little.

After church on Sunday, I spend the day with the kids in the library, organizing books and playing board games. I meet Paul and Stephanie, the two missionaries living at Imani, and like them immediately. I have never met a real missionary, and whatever I thought one would be like is nothing like what Paul and Stephanie really are. I tell them that I want to return—I now know it with certainty—and they are supportive and tell me the list of elders I'll need to ask permission from.

The fast, for what it's worth, is a bust. I faint by the time I hit Leviticus. The fast is over, my decision made.

Lara is still on the mountain and knows none of this.

When she returns and I tell her about the strange series of events, it is settled. After a year of living for ourselves, a year in which we realized daily how lucky we are, coming to an orphanage and seeing need has surely impacted us in no small way. The nature of the idea at all—and Lara's simple enthusiasm—is no small testament to this. We leave Imani knowing we will be back in a few months' time, following the Christmas holidays.

A couple weeks after leaving, we contact Reverend Mathu and the Imani elders to confirm the dates of our return and ask what they think might be useful for us to do while we're there. Lara and I had already decided that we wanted to train for a particular marathon in Kenya during our stay—the only one in the world on a wildlife reserve—and so are floored when they bring up the idea of an after-school running program. We love the idea immediately.

The kids at Imani, we know, are desperate for extracurricular programming. As orphan care experts can explain, once the basic needs of food and clothes and schooling are met, it's easy to forget how important nourishing activities can be in helping to develop traumatized children into healthy adolescents. At the same time, we know the elders at Imani are passionate about ensuring the children have activities to do. The less idle time they have, the less likely they are to fall into trouble or become overwhelmed by their pasts. We begin to think that we could train some of the older adolescents along with us for the marathon. We write letters telling friends and family about what we're doing, asking for visitors, donations to Imani, and running shoes.

By the time we arrive back in Kenya, we have some donated funds, several hundred pairs of running shoes, and a conviction: we will run.

SAMMY

CHAPTER 6

I am glad to have finished my primary school studies and the KCPE secondary school entrance exam and am waiting to hear my scores to see if I can go on to secondary school. There is a two-month waiting period to find out, and I don't have much to do except sit and worry.

One day I am putting some clothes out to dry on the lawn after washing when I see that the door to the library is open. This intrigues me, and I go to the door and see kids inside. This isn't a normal day for the library to be open, so I happily walk in to borrow a book.

Upon entering, I see at the head of the table a white girl, a mzungu, with yellow bangs—or, as I call them at the time, "the things in front of the eyes." She is reading a book to the little kids about David and Goliath. When I see that it is a Christian book, I am particularly interested, because I like these kinds of stories. I also want to know about this new face in the orphanage.

I sit down to listen. She is speaking very slowly and clearly in English, and as I listen I begin interrupting her to ask questions. As the little ones look on, we start talking about things: the United States, education, books, English, technology, and Obama. For some reason, she is very intrigued with the fact that I know about Obama, whom we see on the news in Kenya and I read about when I see a newspaper.

Afterward we go for dinner. It is githeri day, and I learn that this girl has never had the maize and bean mixture before. She asks for salt, and I happily run to the kitchen to get some, because it means that I will get salt also! Usually they don't allow salt for us.

After dinner, I ask her name, and she tells me it is Claire. The next day I don't see Claire, but I am still happy I have made a friend. Even if she will leave, like all visitors.

A few days later it comes for us: our rite of passage.

After graduating from eighth grade in Kenya, young men are circumcised. In the Kikuyu tribe, circumcision is a tradition that means we change from boys into men.

In Kikuyu, every young man must be circumcised. Any young men who are not circumcised are called *kihii*, a derogatory term no one ever wants to hear in reference to themselves.

As I have been taught, circumcision is a cultural moment that teaches us to be strong—not just physically but mentally as well. While we endure the pain, we learn important life lessons.

I am told that it is time for my age group to enter into our circumcision program at the nearby Presbyterian parish. There is a church service to get us prepared for the event, and that night we have a delicious dinner and pray hard. This is where I first meet a man named Mr. Avery, the director of the program. He is smart and well built and one of the first men I ever come to look up to.

Along with my friends from Imani, we enter the program with fifty other boys our age. That first night I see boys around me everywhere doing things that kihiis—uncircumcised boys—would do. They cry, they scream, they beg to be passed over. Not things that real men do. Over the next two days we know that all of us boys will be crying like no other.

The next day the first group is taken at 5:00 a.m. When they return, I see the grief on their faces. They are walking very, very slowly, and I begin to get extremely scared. When 8:00 comes, it is my turn. I enter the small matatu minibus to go to the hospital, and on the way the driver jokes, "Hey, boys, you might want to respect me because I will be the one driving you back." We don't know what he means until he hits the curvy, bumpy part of the road, and we start to wonder how we'll be able to handle this road on the way back when we are in pain and bleeding.

We don't know what is going to happen, and we are afraid. When we get to the hospital, I see five people waiting in line ahead of me. Five people between me and the door. Beyond that door, I know, is pain.

I become very scared, and this is when Mr. Avery, the director of the program and a man I had instantly respected, calls me over. He tells me his life philosophy—that bad and painful moments come and go, and they are all part of the life we are called to live. The best thing we can do is deal with everything as well as possible. When I sit down, I ponder these words and find myself growing calmer.

Soon there are only four people left, then three, then two, then one. Then it is my turn. As I walk through the door, I know there is no going back.

Inside, the nurse puts me in a surgery room where there is another person being operated on. As I listen to the screams, I realize that forty-five minutes have passed. I cannot stop imagining what is going on in there. Then they bring me through the curtain. I lie down on the bed, and they tell me to take off my clothes. I see the doctor take a syringe and put some medicine in it. There is a first burst of terrible hurt and then forty-five minutes more of a horrific, dull, endless pain.

When it is finished, I am so glad. I remember having asked if it would hurt, and now I know the answer. It is very, very painful. As I walk outside, I have to walk like I am riding on a horse. I can't wear my underwear, so I put it in my pocket. When we get back on the bus, I remember that we now have to go back on that horrible road.

The next two days feel like torture.

For two weeks we live in the dorms at a nearby church, taking men's classes and learning about life, HIV and AIDS, high school, and hygiene. Then we are moved to another nearby orphanage to recover for a few more weeks. The orphanage, Upendo, was started by the same Reverend Mathu who started Imani, but it is much smaller and not nearly as nice. There are many disabled children who live here, and it is a good place for us to stay because it has extra rooms.

At Upendo, we eat some of the best food of my life. It is around Christmastime, so there are many visitors and lots of festivity. The month is filled with new friends and wonderful fun. It is also during this time that I realize I can dance!

On January 3, once the holidays are over, we are supposed to return to Imani. Just as planned, Reverend Mathu (Guka) comes to tell us it is time to leave. But I am not ready to return to Imani. I have learned so much in the past few weeks of living there about what it means to live with true kindness. Living with disabled children who take care of each other, even though they are only children themselves, has opened my eyes. But I have heard that every end is a new beginning, and I return to Imani with the hope that this is true.

When we arrive back at Imani, I have mixed feelings. I am happy to be here, where I have lived for a year, but sad to leave my new home of just a few weeks. When I come back, I find there are new faces at the orphanage, and I quickly make some new friends. One friend who will prove to be very important in my life is Hezron. About my age, he is a little taller, more slender, and less dark than me.

That night as I sit to eat my portion of githeri, feelings of sadness and happiness fill me all at once. I realize that I really want to live at Upendo, not Imani, and so the next morning I will go to Eunice, Imani's manager, to tell her what I want to do.

Eunice is one of those women you look up to from the moment you meet her. You don't have a choice in loving her, because she takes care of you as if you were her own son or daughter. She is smart and knows exactly what children need. When Eunice was first contracted as the new Imani Children's Home manager, most of us kids at Imani were not very welcoming of the idea. We did not see why we would need her when we had two other matrons to help us, and it seemed she would simply deal with administrative issues for Imani's elders. We were used to things happening in a different way, and we resisted the change.

But because Eunice is very funny and a respected church member of the PCEA, she started winning our hearts immediately. As a musician, she revived the choir program, and we would regularly go to learn songs and sing them during church events. In this way, many of us would also spend more time with her.

As the days have gone by, students have spent more and more time in her office, asking questions about new rules and talking about problems at school, even going to her when they are feeling depressed and need encouragement. As a teacher, she also helps us with our English class, our English homework, and any subjects we are struggling with. She knows how to handle young people and adults alike, and we all respect her greatly.

Eunice also acts as a mediator with the matrons and the kids; she is just like a big bridge between the two groups. Every time something goes wrong between the matrons and the kids, she is there making sure that both parties can come to an agreement and respect each other. Until that point, there was no one to go to, since we often felt intimidated by the elders like Cucu and Guka, whom we respected so much. We needed someone we were much closer to, someone like Eunice, who would be able to solve our conflicts.

She also started a Bible study group that I have come to love. Since it meets at 5:00 a.m.—an hour before we normally wake—I sometimes oversleep. But whenever I do go, I feel close to God.

I didn't get to know Eunice personally until I became friends with her daughter, who is in her twenties. She sometimes comes to visit on the weekends and stays with Eunice in the apartment on the second floor of the orphanage. Eunice's daughter is funny and never looks at us like we are weird kids; she looks at us like we are her brothers and sisters.

Over time, I've realized that Eunice is one of the smartest people I have ever met—eloquent and seemingly very young. She looks like she is forty years old, but one day when I asked her how old she was, she told me she was fifty-two! At first I thought she was a liar, but then I realized it was true.

Eunice—or "Manager," as we call her—is one of my African heroes.

After my afternoon duties the next day, I go to the manager's office and she tells me to sit down. She asks me how I am feeling. I tell her I am okay, but I think I'd be better off if I lived at Upendo, not at Imani. Kindly, she explains to me that what I want is not possible. When I question this—"But there are rooms available to live in! We stayed in them!"—she says that people at Upendo Children's Home more than likely have had fewer chances in life than people at Imani Children's Home, and we need to keep the space open for those kinds of people to get the special attention they need. She reminds me that many people would like to have the chance to be at Imani but do not have it, so I should be grateful for the opportunity I have.

At the time, I am young and don't understand the chance I have been given or the chance that Upendo gives to many disabled kids. So when I leave the manager's office, I am stomping mad, asking myself over and over, "Why won't she just let me leave?"

When my friend Hezron sees me, he asks me, "Sammy, why were you in there with Manager?"

When I explain to him that I want to live at Upendo, he asks me a question. "Sammy, why are you here at Imani?"

I answer dumbly that I don't have a choice. "I am here to live!" I say.

And then he tells me, "Then do it! Live!"

He reminds me that people like us often do not have lots of choices. Instead, we take what we are given. He reminds me that I have a chance to be in a great orphanage that provides me with food, a place to sleep, and a chance to gain the discipline I need in life.

This is when I realize something about us as orphans. When life throws us a lemon, we must take as much juice from it as we can, because we don't know when it might be taken away. I realize this is true not just for orphans but for all people. When life gives you that lemon, take as much juice as you can, because you don't know when the lemon will be taken away and you will be left without any fruit at all.

In January, schools start reopening in Kenya. However, first-year high school students—Form One students—start school in February. So we stay in the orphanage for a month before school starts, waiting for the KCPE results that will determine if we can go to secondary school. This gives me time to get to know the few new friends and faces at Imani that will be my family for the next four years.

In Kenya, when you finish the KCPE exam, you wait for your scores to see if you can continue on to secondary school or if your future will be to leave school or maybe learn a trade instead. If you don't get the invite, it's very bad, and even though I pray hard for a letter, nothing arrives. Some of my friends receive letters, but I still haven't heard anything.

Finally, the manager calls me into her office one day. I find out my score—304 out of 500, which I think is pretty good—and I get a letter from Giakombe, the local secondary school next door to the orphanage. I jump up and down, saying, "It's something! It's something!"

A few days later the students are called in to have measurements taken for the school uniform. At first I think it is a joke and am reluctant to go. "New clothes? Yeah, right!" But then the seamstresses send for me again and I know they are serious! I go upstairs and meet a wonderful Christian lady who takes my measurements. And as she does, I realize I am about to start a new life. Am I ready for it?

During this season, I am really afraid. For the first four months of Form One, life is not the easiest. In Kenya, we have something called monolization. It comes from the word *mono*, meaning "one," for Form One. Monolization, or mono, is bullying to the extreme and makes life a nightmare. Most upper-class students in Forms Two, Three, and Four don't really think of it as bullying but rather as a form of payback for what happened to them when they were in Form One. Because they were monolized, they pay it back by monolizing other people. And this cycle goes on and on and doesn't stop.

The worst cases of monolizing, as we learn during our circumcision class, happen to boys who are not circumcised or boys from a different nationality. Let's say you're not a Kikuyu like I am but a Luo attending school in a Kikuyu community. That makes it even worse. There are stories where a Form One student is sent to the market by an upperclassman and told he must return with red jam, margarine, tea, milk, and fifty shillings in change. And he's only given ten shillings! If he does not satisfy the impossible requirements, he may have to wash the clothes or the lunch and dinner dishes of that upperclassman for a whole year. Basically, the upperclassman will make the Form One student a slave if he doesn't satisfy the demands.

Sometimes Form One students are beaten up or bullied. Since my brother is in Form Three, I know he will help me, but I am still afraid. I know that life isn't always fair, and mono is just one little example of that. Sometimes, I have come to learn, you just have to deal with whatever you are handed. A better future is about the way we handle the situations we face—and the better we handle them, the better our results will be. In life, things come and go. It's our duty to be satisfied with the results we have after our situations pass. I know this and am determined to start my life in high school—mono and all.

By February I am ready to start secondary school with all my other counterparts: Kevin, Kahuria, Njoki, Maggie, Jane, Marion, Joyce, and many more. A lot of my new classmates are people I have seen from time to time in the streets of the village but who have not yet entered my life. Now I will spend the next four years with them.

As we start classes, we also begin to take on the new customs of high school. On our first day of high school when the teacher enters the room, we all stand up because it is a habit from primary school, but the teacher quickly explains that we don't need to do that anymore. New things are everywhere—new buildings to enter and new subjects to learn. We get new books and test booklets and are introduced to all kinds of new clubs. Hezron and I decide to join Scouts, and we also start eating lunch at school—which I find fun!

I soon get the hang of things. Wake up at 6:00 a.m. on the days where there is no 5:00 a.m. Bible study, have breakfast at 6:30, be at school by 7:00, eat lunch at 1:40, leave school at 5:00, come home, have tea, wash my clothes, do my duties, have dinner at 6:00, watch the news, then head off to study hall until 10:30, when it is time for bed. This becomes my new routine.

And then, a few weeks later, the white girl who had asked me about Obama comes back to stay and changes everything.

When Claire and Lara come back, they bring a new friend with them—a man named Jonathan who likes to play the guitar and stays a few weeks.

At first I don't recognize Claire because she doesn't have bangs. Then one day when I am coming home from school I pass by Claire, who is sitting on a chair on the veranda, playing with the kids. She stops me and says, "Hey, aren't you Sammy?"

"Yes, yes I am," I say.

She asks me, "Aren't you in Standard Eight?"

I can't believe what she has just said, and all my friends start laughing hysterically. What Claire doesn't know is that she has insulted me badly, saying I am still in Standard Eight when I have actually just started Form One. Essentially, this means she is calling me a kihii—an uncircumcised person. In Kikuyu culture, when we haven't been circumcised, we are considered boys. To us, a kihii is not worthy of being called a man. But when we undergo circumcision, like I did the week after I first met Claire a few months earlier, we are considered men due to the pain we endure. Being a kihii in a Kikuyu community when you're no longer a small boy is a bad thing, and if someone calls you that it means they have no respect for you. It is like calling a black person the N-word. It hurts and is very disrespectful.

To me, Claire has committed one of the crimes of the century. I vow never to speak to her again, and I keep my distance.

And I'm not the only one.

When Claire and Lara move into the apartment at Imani, most of the kids are skeptical. Claire and Lara are much younger than everyone else who has ever come to live at Imani Children's Home. Any of the teenagers or young people we have seen come over the years have only stayed for a few days, and no one can understand why seemingly young white people, or mzungus, want to come to live with us. Slowly, though, I begin to hear that Claire and Lara are starting a running program. Since Hezron is really interested in it, I get excited about it too.

A lot of people sign up for the first practice. We do a lot of weird stretches and some games, mostly for the little kids, who can't run much. Many people are just there to watch.

The second practice I go to, though, is different. We do a 5K run and follow it with some stretches. There are a lot fewer people, and things are calmer. There is an early practice with games for the younger kids, and then the older kids are able to do a real training run. Whenever I go, I get the chance to talk to Lara. By and by, I start talking to Claire as well. I realize that in life you're going to meet people who are going to make you angry without the intent of doing so, especially when they come from different cultures. Tolerance and forgiveness are of the utmost importance when someone doesn't know everything about your culture. Instead, it's your responsibility to teach them or show them what your culture means.

So I decide to ignore what Claire said, because even though it was painful, Claire seems like an awesome person. Although that incident now seems very petty, at the time it helped me discover one of the skills I have in life, which is to forgive others. We all hurt people. When you think about it, if every person you have ever wronged—knowingly or unknowingly—never forgave you, that would make you feel very bad. So we must learn to forgive, even when white girls call us kihiis.

Little by little, the running program helps many of the kids get to know Lara and Claire better, and we all start spending more time with them outside of practice. They know more of our names, and they start learning some Swahili. They are also really funny, and we all laugh that they have the same kind of humor we do. They call all the little kids "crazy" and "troublemaker," and they trust we are smart enough to understand their jokes. Slowly, everyone starts to see they are more like us than we realize.

One Saturday I go for a run. Lara is running also, and she is really sweaty and dirty. When I come close to her, I can tell she is stinking and she needs a shower—she really needs one! That's when I realize that there's nothing special about people who look different; we really are all the same. Lara is stinking and sweating just as much as any Kenyan does.

To be honest, when Claire and Lara came and lived with us, they changed our perception of what mzungus were. Until then, and with only a few exceptions, we hadn't really liked mzungus much. To us, mzungus just represented money. When they came, all they did was look down on us and feel sorry for us. Then they would sign a check and leave it with the manager.

When Lara and Claire came, they were different. They used a different resource than money. They stayed with us and showed us that they're the same as we are.

SAMMY

CHAPTER 7

Along with the new running program, Claire and Lara bring something special for us. They bring us shoes.

At the time, only about three or four kids at Imani have proper sports shoes. Most of us run on bare feet or in our black heavy school shoes, which ends up ruining the shoes very fast.

One Saturday morning my friend Hezron and I are coming back from doing duties in the garden when we find out that we are all going to be given a brand-new pair of shoes. It turns out that when Claire and Lara left Kenya the first time, they went back to the United States and did a shoe collection, and now they are giving us the shoes.

In the afternoon they start passing out the shoes, starting with the little kids and working their way up. When it comes time for my turn, Lara takes me by the hand. Claire is busy helping other people fit their feet into the shoes and is dealing with many complaints from students who say their shoes don't fit or their shoes aren't good enough.

Lara helps me try on different pairs of shoes to find a pair that fits well enough. The problem is that I have long, thin feet and can't find the right ones. She eventually gives me a pair that almost fits. I don't like them, though, and leave with a sad face. They aren't shiny or good-looking like some others that I see. Like everyone else, I want so badly to look good and to have shoes and clothes that look the best they absolutely can, since I don't have much.

I know I'm not the only one trying to get better shoes, and I also know that Claire and Lara may not understand and may think this doesn't make sense. I can hear them asking themselves inside their heads, *If they don't have any shoes, why do they not just take what they can get?*

But it is just the way I feel—and the way many other students feel that day. We want to have the best pair of shoes so we can look our best with the little we have.

Lara tries to tell me that the shoes she chose for me are in fashion in America, but I won't budge. I see some dark sneakers I like and ask Lara if I can have them. Lara says I can only if they fit. She puts the shoes on my feet, and they fit—barely. I can walk in them, but I know I will never be able to run in them. When she asks if they fit—and if I have a little bit of space in the front for running—I lie, and she lets me walk off with my new dark sneakers. I walk out of the room that Saturday with my sneakers tied around my chest, giving them kisses.

The next day, Sunday, everyone goes to breakfast as usual. After breakfast, it is time for church, and as we walk in, Claire and Lara see that all 170 of us are wearing our new sneakers along with our fanciest church clothes. Claire and Lara cannot believe it, and I can see their eyes sparkling with water drops. It is a special moment for them.

On Monday we have running practice. Lara and Claire come for the run as usual, and they are surprised when they see that almost no one is wearing their new shoes, even though they had just worn them to church the day before! Instead, everyone is in bare feet or school shoes. Like the other kids, I don't want to wear my new shoes to go running because I want to keep them new and pretty as long as possible.

As part of Hope Runs, which is the name of the nonprofit organization they have started to support the running program, Claire and Lara have worked to get funding to put a few dozen runners in a marathon many months from now. Because Hezron and I have been showing up to the new running program every day and practicing hard, we are chosen to take part in the marathon.

As we start training for the marathon—and they do make us wear our shoes!—our practices are taken to a whole new level, and we start running long and hard, up to thirty kilometers in one day, as we prepare for the forty-two kilometer marathon. As we run, I often get to the point where I almost stop when my muscles run out of energy, but then I keep going. Hezron always encourages me, telling me never to stop and to keep pushing.

I can see now that this team and the practices we have teach me a lot about life. Sometimes things can get hard—really, really hard—but your dedication and enthusiasm can keep you going. There are always moments in the race when you are tired and can't move one more step. But you do, and you keep yourself going because there is a prize at the end. You keep running.

It's the same thing in life. Like in the marathon training, when things get hard, you keep going.

Over the years I have seen visitors come to Imani with cameras, and I have always wanted to touch one. I would watch them take pictures or take video, and I would dream of one day holding that machine.

Then one day Lara is just wandering around Imani filming, and I decide to ask. Lara and Claire and I are close friends by now, and we talk and laugh every day. Curious, like any boy curious about a camera, I ask Lara about it. She starts explaining the camera to me, its functions, and what it does. Then, at last, she asks me if I want to touch it.

I cannot believe my ears and look at her with confusion. "Are you serious?" Then I put my hands together to hold the camera.

She tells me one thing: "Take care of it; it's my baby." I assure her that I will, and she puts the camera in my hands.

As she gives me the camera, I feel a strange kind of joy. Like the joy you feel when your team makes a goal in overtime or when the shot just barely enters the hoop. That kind of joy.

I take the camera and start looking through it, and it's as if I can see the world with whole new eyes.

There aren't words to describe all my feelings in that moment, and why the camera is so important to me. To this day I'm not sure how crazy Lara must have been to let me use it, but she did. From then on, I keep waiting for the next moment I can touch a camera again.

After many months of Claire and Lara living at Imani, their work begins to be recognized all over the world. We are told that some special writers from a magazine called *Runner's World* are coming to Imani for a week to do some interviews and to take pictures of the children training with Hope Runs. Apparently, people in other places think that Claire and Lara are doing an awesome thing in coming to an orphanage and giving us opportunities to engage in something extracurricular like running.

We are asked to go for a run one day with our shoes on so that the cameraman can take pictures. When we go out on the road, I find out that some people don't have their shoes on and are still running barefoot. Years later I see one of the pictures taken that day of one of the kids who wasn't wearing shoes—it is an awesome photo, but I'm not sure it was what *Runner's World* expected! That day we all run the regular 5K loop as we normally do, and the cameraman takes photos along the way.

When we all return to the orphanage, Claire and Lara call me and my friend Mwaniki aside. They tell us we are going to do some more photos, just the four of us, so this time we all get into the cameraman's car and drive along the 5K loop. This is the first time I've ever been in someone's personal car—I had been in a few minibuses before, like when I went for the circumcision on that bumpy road—and I sit in the backseat, smiling to myself and thinking, *I'm in a real car!*

The cameraman has Lara and Claire do some modeling, and I think they look very beautiful and better than they normally look when we run! Then he starts taking pictures of Mwaniki and me as well.

When we come back, I am excited and start talking to the other students about it, but then I see they are not happy at all. Some are very mad at us, and I realize they are jealous that Mwaniki and I were especially invited to go take more photos, which I did not think of beforehand. Of all the students in the program, we were called out by Claire and Lara. We say to them we were chosen because we had been so diligent in our running, and this is true. But I know in my heart we have a special relationship, and soon people will start to see that.

Finally, the month comes for the big marathon, which we are running at a place called the Lewa Wildlife Conservancy with thousands of other people from different countries. We have a few weeks left, and everyone is really enthusiastic and ready for the race.

Even Claire and Lara are excited, and when I talk to them, I see their eyes are full of happiness. They know the running program has gone well, many students have improved their times, and many little kids who aren't running the marathon have learned to like running. We have also become close friends, which makes me glad, because there was a time when I had been very mad at Claire and hadn't wanted anything to do with her! Now I often knock on the door of their apartment when I need advice, or want to talk about something, or need help with chemistry or writing, or anytime, really. And, of course, when something interesting is happening and I need to ask for the video camera to tape it!

The Tuesday a few weeks before the marathon, there is a soft rain falling, and Claire and Lara tell us we have to be at practice on time because there is a big announcement. Everyone is excited because we know it has to do with the Lewa Marathon, and we can't wait to hear what it is. I get there early and have on my nice shoes, running shorts, and shirt. Hezron is with me at the time, and when we arrive, Claire and Lara seem hesitant to tell us anything. I can sense something is wrong, and finally, they tell us that it looks like some of us will not be able to run the marathon.

We cannot believe our ears. *What!?* This news seems impossible to us. Haven't we all been practicing for months to go to this amazing event? Going to the marathon means a lot to us. Most of all, I think, because it is a chance to travel—to get out of our enclosed orphanage life and the small village and to see a bit of Kenya. The Lewa Marathon is the chance to do that.

Lara and Claire have to explain the whole story, and I can see it saddens them. It turns out that anyone younger than seventeen years old will no longer be able to participate due to the rules of the race. This kills me, because Hezron and I are part of that age group. We simply cannot believe it. After all our hard work, after months of practice, we have been told we cannot participate.

We are angry, and we go back to the dormitory and stay there that night. We don't go up to the study hall and we don't talk to anyone; we just keep saying the same thing over and over to each other: "This is not fair."

The next day Claire brings the few of us together who can no longer run and says she is very sorry about what has happened, but we will definitely still go to the race to spectate.

Then we realize, "Wait! This is perfect! We're going to go for a trip, but we don't have to run and exhaust ourselves!" We are immediately happy again and can't wait for the race.

The night before the race, the runners leave to make the long drive. They are staying overnight at a hostel near the race grounds so that they can get to the starting line early in the morning. The rest of us kids from Imani are leaving early the next day with Matron and Cucu and arriving a couple hours later.

During that night's Friday worship, we ask God for safe travels for all. We pray that the runners will be safe in their hostel and get sleep so they can start the run on the right foot.

At 4:30 a.m. that Sunday, Hezron wakes me up to get ready to go to the marathon. We have breakfast, and soon everyone is ready to climb on the enormous bus. The bus is beautiful, and from the moment we step on board I know this is going to be a truly amazing experience. As the gates of Imani open and we pass through, I gaze out. I've walked on that same road so many times but have never really gotten a sense of the area and the surrounding community. As we leave the village and then Nyeri town and head out on the open road all the way around Mount Kenya, I cannot cease to see the wonders of this beautiful place.

We travel for more than six hours, passing amazingly different, adventurous landscapes. Cucu and Matron have joined us to make sure we are safe and well, and we love having them there to support us.

When we arrive at Lewa, I see that it is a nice morning for a race. It is cool and cloudy with a nice breeze. I imagine how grateful the runners are for the weather, since it is normally such a hot place with lots of dust, and it hasn't rained in a long while.

I soon notice that there are a lot of people from the Masai tribe in Lewa. This is new for me, because back in Nyeri there are almost none. That said, people always think my middle name, Ikua, is a Masai name, since it sounds so unusual for a Kikuyu name. I have heard so many people say I must secretly be Masai that I had started to believe it, and I am glad to see "my people" all around, selling food and water. I also see some mzungus, and then I start to see people from other cultures entirely. It is amazing to think that everyone is here for this one event.

Hezron and I immediately start walking around, making friends. When people speak English, we speak English. When people speak Swahili, we speak Swahili. At some point I lose Hezron in the mountain of faces, and as I walk around alone, I start making friends with some of the Masai who live in the area and herd cattle.

I soon wander back to the area where all the other kids from the orphanage are watching the race, waiting for people we know to cross the finish line so we can cheer for them. I see a television camera for a national news station pointed toward me, and I am really happy to know we'll be on TV! I didn't realize I had been standing right in front of the place where the world-record holders are finishing the marathon. They run so fast for so long, I simply cannot believe my eyes.

I start cheering for anyone I see finishing while I wait, so I am really thrilled when finally some people from Imani start crossing the line. At first it is all boys. I see Wilson and then Ewoi both pushing their hardest. We all shout and scream when they pass through, and I think about what a great thing it is to see my friends from the orphanage in an international race like this. I shout so, so loud.

I eat a delicious sandwich for lunch, and then we go back on the bus to start our journey back to Imani. The one day we have been away feels so long. As we are driving back, I see the scenes of the day in my head, playing forward and backward and forward again. It is really like I am seeing them fresh, not like I have ever seen them before.

CLAIRE

CHAPTER 8

It was inevitable, of course, that Lara would get sick. When important things happened to Lara, she got fevers. The night before we graduated from Stanford, she was feverish in her parents' hotel room, shivering under weighty down blankets.

"Maybe it's time to take an aspirin," I suggested.

"Humph," she responded, part delirious, part defiant. Lara, now almost a doctor, hates taking medicine.

In Kenya, the conditions in the weeks leading up to the marathon prove optimal for a soaring fever. Daily disasters increase tenfold, and every few minutes some small child or marathon-training teen knocks on our door with a different impending crisis. The children, not knowing what this marathon entails or if we may disappear as soon as it is over like all the other white people who come, lose all sense of perspective with their problems. Nothing is too small or too large for our immediate intervention. We complain hourly that we even lack the time to develop an appropriate triage system for what has clearly become a failure of management.

Small children coming into the kitchen to fight over who can take our compost to the cows becomes one of many loud interruptions to our tenuous conference calls with London about thousands of dollars in marathon fees. From the children's transportation to their accommodations to their safety, the weight of the responsibility seems ready to topple us.

And yet the children have their priorities. Every five minutes or so during any relatively free time the children have, they knock on our door.

One day we hear the familiar knock for the umpteenth time.

"They want more paper," Lara correctly assesses. Ever since we started providing kids with paper to write letters to their US prayer partners, we haven't had a moment of peace. Our supplies are dwindling, and so is our patience. All day and all night they want paper.

I get up and crack the front door.

"Give me paper," Mercy says in her trademark tubercular rasp. Mercy was the first child in the orphanage known to be sick with HIV/AIDS and has been getting steadily healthier in the year since she arrived, but she is still very small for her age. Everyone treats her like a baby sister, carrying her everywhere unnecessarily and doting on her to no end.

I begin the bargaining. "We can't give you paper, Mercy. You never wrote a letter. We only give paper to people who write letters."

"Here is letter."

"This is not your letter, Mercy. Someone *else* wrote this."

"Here is letter two."

"This is not your letter either, Mercy. Go write your own letter on your own piece of paper."

Momentarily silenced, she retreats. Ten minutes later she's back, knocking.

"Give me paper."

"Mercy," I reason, "you are not writing letters. Mercy, they are *using* you for paper."

She stares at me blankly, blinking her big brown eyes.

"We cannot give you paper," I assert.

"Letter for Mary?" she tries.

"Which Mary?" I test her.

"Mary Waithera."

I snort. "We already gave Mary Waithera letter paper today."

She tries again. "Mary Wanguru."

"Tell her I gave all the Marys paper today!" Lara yells from the other room.

"Letter?"

"One letter paper per day per person, Mercy," I say, closing the door.

"Give me paper."

"Goodbye, Mercy."

Twenty minutes later she's back, knocking plaintively.

"Mercy, I am not answering the door!" I say loudly.

"Paper. Give me paper."

"Go away, Mercy."

Her fingers are under the door now, grasping the air.

"Letter?"

In contrast to Mercy, Little Mary—whom we have taken to calling Chula, or *frog* in Swahili—has mastered the actual art of letter writing. (Due to Kenyans' transposing of the *l* and *r* sounds, the kids believe *Lara* is written *Roola* and *Claire* is *Crayol*. By the same token, it is not until years later that we learn *frog* in Swahili is actually spelled *chura*.) When Lara's parents were in Kenya the month before, Mary had written them a letter.

Dear Roola Mother and Father,
    I miss you I pray for you. I am Mary Waithera and I am
9 years old.
    I am in Standard 2 and I live at Imani Children's Home.
I am a frog.
    I miss you I pray for you,

Mary

We were notably impressed.

"You are Chula now," we told her.

"Like Celtel?" she said.

At the time, the most useless technician in the world, from the phone company Celtel, was at Imani every other day. Much like the plumber at Imani, who is a friend of the reverend and thus cannot be fired, the Celtel employee's only apparent strength was in reliably disabling all electrical outlets and internet connections. He is also named Chula.

"Yes, Mary, like Celtel."

One day Mary can't believe it when I tell her Lara is napping because she is sick. "Roola is sleeping? For running?"

"Come look, Chula," I say. I take Mary into Lara's room, where it is dark, and I tell her to sit on the bed. The bed moves. She squeals.

"It is Roola!"

As we near the marathon, the training runs become even more grueling. The little children who are too small to run long distances have the important job of being cheerers, which means they are tasked with passing out water and snacks. They never fail to consume more than they distribute. A marathon training run of up to eighteen or twenty miles means up to six loops on the road around the orphanage, giving us an effective cheering station in front of the orphanage that allows these little kids to be kept safe by the home and yet also be passed by the runners many times. The jobs for manning the cheering station are seen as desperately important. Usually Edwin, nine, rules the gaggle of other nine-year-olds as a benevolent but patronizing snack station overlord.

After getting water for the runners in buckets and borrowing a number of brown plastic cups from the kitchen, the cheerers also have the duty of ensuring that the mzungu water is kept separately in the mzungu water bottles. It never goes without comment that the poor mzungus are so pathetic that they cannot drink African water.

"Special water!" Edwin yells when we pass, pointing out the particular bottles just for "Roola" and "Crayol."

In reality, we had to campaign long and hard to make the runners drink water in the beginning. They told us if you were hot from running and drank cool water you would die, then looked at us like we were idiots when we expressed skepticism. We even brought in a famous Kenyan runner who was from the area for a motivational talk, in which we urged him to center on the importance of drinking water. It didn't work. Eventually, as training runs grew longer, physiology won out and the runners started to drink. Barely.

Things have progressed, and now the runners frequently inform us that water is second rate, and they all are convinced that true runners only drink glucose, a sugary electrolyte drink. But it is overpriced at the Indian supermarket, so I found a homemade energy drink recipe online on a day that Chula from Celtel wasn't working. The recipe consisted of food coloring, tea, salt, and sugar, so I brought some of the cheerers in the kitchen before the long training run, and we mixed up buckets of the purple stuff along with a garbage bag full of "popcorns." The cheerers tasted the drink in the kitchen and provided feedback.

"It is like the dirt."

For children with a massive sweet tooth and no access to sugar, this was a statement.

"That's the foulest thing I've ever had in my life," Lara offered. I gave it to Sammy, and he agreed, making exaggerated retching noises.

Back to water, I thought. Water that the Kenyans barely drank anyway.

As long as nothing else remotely interesting is happening, the cheerers can be counted on to sit manning the water station for five hours as boys, girls, and Lara and I run the loops. They refill the water dutifully, and Edwin, in his floor-length purple down jacket—regardless of the weather—takes his job particularly seriously.

"I give the cups," he says, chin held high.

"Edwin, you are ridiculous," I respond in turn.

"I have drunk," he says, referencing the water he sips far more than he passes out. Given the constant wars to force water drinking, Edwin is the most hydrated Kenyan I know.

"That was very good English, Edwin."

He smiles, his belly sticking out in pride.

On days when there are cookies or oranges or popcorn to give out, such items cannot be left anywhere near the cheerers unless Lara or I am around.

"More popcorn for me?" station manager Edwin yells as the runners come by every five kilometers.

"No! For runners!" we pant back.

A week before the marathon, a fever coming on, Lara is perched on her bed with her head out the window, the only place with reception. The man in London is saying he cannot possibly manage to help all the people asking for reductions in marathon fees.

"That's eighty dollars per Kenyan and four hundred dollars

The first known picture of Lara (left) and Claire, freshman year at Stanford University. Matching J.Crew jean jackets, of course.

Claire finishes the Madrid marathon on her and Lara's first stop around the world.

Claire on a camel for their overnight stay in the desert in Morocco. Sandstorm imminent.

Frank Vogel

Shot from above the
orphanage.

The shop across the dirt road
from the orphanage. Claire
and Lara are still unclear
on what the Tabby Mult
Complex Retail Shop sells.

Frank Vogel

The orphanage gardens.

Jonathan Finns

A secondary school classroom at Sammy's high school in Kenya.

Claire at the dining table/desk in the orphanage apartment, aka Hope Runs headquarters.

Claire walking with some of the girls through the orphanage compound.

Sammy, fifteen, at the finish line of the Lewa Marathon. (He was filming, not running.)

The Lewa Marathon finishers. After months of training, every teen who started the race finished it! They slept all the way back to the orphanage.

The orphanage dining hall stands in the center of the orphanage grounds, and its interior and exterior spaces prove a hotspot for Friday worship, clothes drying, soccer games, and general mayhem.

Sammy on his first day of sophomore year at MCI. He begged for maps on his walls.

Sammy and his favorite teacher and resident advisor, Declan Galvin, who knows Swahili and had studied in Kenya. Declan would remain in Sammy's life for years and would eventually return to Kenya himself to write his PhD dissertation.

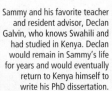

Sammy was named prom king at MCI his senior year. In his first dance he's smiling wide.

Sammy making cookies in California after Lara moves to start Stanford Medical School. He wishes he could put cheese in them.

Claire and José in Yosemite, where they travel for José to meet Claire's family.

Sammy giving a reading at Claire's wedding, which took place in one of the oldest churches in Buenos Aires.

At Claire's wedding, her friend, Twitter colleague and wedding photographer Jillian West, did a wonderful series of shots of wedding party members in a claw-footed bathtub. The series now hangs in Claire's guest bathroom. When Sammy got in the tub with Lara (left) and Claire (right), he said he didn't think this was the sort of wedding picture they took in Kenya.

Sammy giving a toast at Claire and José's wedding rehearsal dinner in Argentina (sparkling grape juice for him).

Jillian West

Lara (left), Sammy, and Claire at Iguazu Falls, where they traveled together after Claire's wedding.

Amalia McGibbon

José Diaz-Ortiz

The "Sammy family" in Ecuador.

José Díaz-Ortiz

Louis, baby Oscar, Lara, Claire, and Sammy outside Sammy's host family's house during his Global Citizen Year.

Sammy in Argentina. He stayed up until all hours of the night talking with the hotel staff, getting them to make him scrambled eggs each morning.

Jillian West

per American!" Lara says into the phone. And then, "I see." As she furiously shakes her head, it doesn't look like she sees at all.

Sprightly Charles, eight, dances by the window in his turquoise pants with laundry soap in hand.

"I will kill you," he sings congenially and then erupts into giggles.

And I think for the millionth time that these children have taken my heart.

"The discount they gave is laughable," Lara says as she hangs up the phone. "And we have another problem."

That night the teens who have been training for weeks sit in a circle as Lara and I hold the contracts they have to fill out for participation in the race. "You are too young," we have to say to a handful of them, including Sammy. It's awful to repeat the words the London man had bellowed at Lara, and we feel even more awful knowing that we simply hadn't thought to look up the rules many months ago. We created this problem, and we know it.

Sammy, whose stick-thin legs and stunted height haven't changed much since I first met him a year earlier, would surely have been the smallest teen to ever cross the finish line. He seems to take the news in stride. He's still on a high from shooting a few videos for *Runner's World* magazine that they put on their website. More importantly, in the eyes of the community, his prowess with the video camera has proclaimed him a professional, and he has been granted access to more than one local wedding, standing on stage in the church and sticking the camera in the bride's and groom's faces as they say their vows. When he finds out that he is too young to run the marathon after all, he pouts but immediately opts for recording the event instead.

On the morning we leave for the marathon, I wake up to find Lara making coffee while James, the shy running captain, lurks awkwardly outside the kitchen window.

"What's he doing?" I ask Lara.

"He's nervous," she says.

"Did you talk to him?"

"He doesn't want to talk."

James had been turned out on the streets at a young age, and only by convincing Imani to take him in had he saved his future. His earnestness made his poor English that much more endearing. When he first heard that *Runner's World* magazine was coming to write about Imani, he told Lara with excitement, "If one day I see the children of Imani in these pages, I will not be able to hide my teeth." Although James is stockier than most Kenyan runners and not as tall as he could have been, his dedication is unmatched, and he is more excited than any other for the race ahead.

By the time we pile into the vans for the marathon the day before the race, half of Imani seems to hate us. By allowing only teenagers to train for the marathon, we inevitably left out dozens of younger, smaller children who might have wanted to run the marathon but simply aren't old enough to do so. For many children, the impetus to train for the marathon may have been less about running than it was about the notion of an organized and supervised activity that comes with the promise of a thrilling trip built in. I had hundreds of sports teams and after-school opportunities to choose from as a child; the Imani kids have none. Understandably, then, it does seem unfair to smaller children that they don't have the chance to participate, and we hate that in giving something to some, we are inevitably creating disappointment for others.

Over the months, one of the most surprising things Lara and I have come to understand about working in an orphanage where any commodity is so valued—whether a field trip or a treasured plastic bag—is that the act of giving is fraught with complications.

At first we were shocked by what ends up being "giveable"—and I don't just mean how the children always root through our trash bags. Time with one of us alone is an incredibly precious resource. One day Lara came into the apartment and burst into tears. She had been drawing with the children, she says, and found herself overwhelmed by how desperate the four small girls were for the briefest of her attentions. "Roola, look I make! Look I draw!" They had clawed at one another to score her glance.

In Kenya, the practice of giving had become one of complete dread for us, and there were few things I had started to look forward to less than personally giving out things. Of course I want the children to have running shoes, and shirts, and shorts, and equipment, but I don't want to handle the guilt and attendant blame of not giving everyone wonderful—and equally wonderful—items. Especially as the value system dictating different degrees of wonderfulness continues to elude Lara and me.

In a home of 170 kids, the squeakiest wheel gets the attention. No matter how egalitarian we try to be, when the resources are limited, there is inevitably a food chain that leaves the most enterprising of the kids closest to the desired resources. Many of the children ended up at Imani because they were adept at looking out for their best interests. And as we saw, the bright ones didn't stop doing this just because they were now living in the relative lap of luxury of the orphanage. When we gave children new shoes, the smart ones pushed their luck and asked for nicer ones. When we gave them an aisle seat on the bus to the race, some children didn't accept our first offer and instead angled for a window. Although this surely annoyed me at times, I respected it, and I recognized that this behavior was hardly new. This is the story of successful humans everywhere.

I have also learned to question the very notion that I am *supposed* to gain pleasure at all from giving out world resources. One could spend a lifetime wondering why my American passport has given me the authority to pass out running shoes to Kenyans.

After months in Africa, I am starting to come full circle with the giving—and perhaps am finally finding a balance in it all. At the first level, it seems that you give of yourself because you want to help. When we started the running program, this is what Lara and I thought. We were running because we wanted to help the children.

On the next level, you realize that what you are giving is mostly just helping you and that you want to help because it makes you feel good. In our case, we saw that we were learning more from the experience of living with these kids than they were learning from us. Our lives were changing more than theirs were.

On the third level—when you are mired in the mess so much that you can't disentangle yourself from a needy population—you realize it doesn't have much to do with want. You simply need to help, whether you want to or not. When I came to Africa, I wanted to give shoes. Then I saw how hard giving was. Now I am learning that giving (whether shoes or schooling or money or mosquito nets or health clinics) is an important responsibility, and it's something that I have the responsibility to learn to do well. My feelings about it don't need to be part of the equation.

And so we faced a decision of whether we should bring any children to cheer on the runners at the race. We once again were pitted as the purveyor of opportunity for some and thus the denier of opportunity for many others. There was nothing we wanted less than making one hundred kids stay at the orphanage while seventy of their peers came on a fancy bus to watch the older kids run a marathon, but it was a simple problem of economics. We did not have the money for more. And so the question remained: do we still take some? Did taking some children to cheer give them a greater chance of one day running that marathon themselves?

In the cold orphanage apartment of a Kenyan June, we went in circles on these issues too many times to count. Although there were occasions in Africa when we gave everyone nothing rather than giving a few people something, we decided that there were times when passing limited resources to smaller numbers of participants was a good idea, even though it was hardly fair. We took the children who had most consistently completed running practice, even after marathon chances had passed (or were never possible if they were young), and we hoped that this was one of those times.

Eunice, the cherished orphanage manager with a secret love for *Desperate Housewives*, comes with us when we set out with the eighteen runners. By the time the two vans pull onto the road, I am on a sweaty vinyl seat next to Mwaniki, the stick-thin poet with the sub-personalities of aspiring model and future car salesman. A couple years older than his sidekick Sammy, Mwaniki says his greatest concern, prerace, is having short enough shorts at the race to make him look like a "true" runner.

"Me, I like the *short* shorts," he had explained to Lara earlier in the week.

Given that we had far too many donated women's running shorts that none of the Kenyan girls were allowed to wear (the elders made them run in knee-length school skirts), we were happy to oblige Mwaniki's fashion concerns.

Mwaniki makes life hysterical yet complex. One time he convened what we thought was a meeting thanking us for training the marathoners and then launched into a well-rehearsed presentation of the flaws in the marathon shirts the runners had been given.

"Exhibit one," he began, numbering his points to ensure that we noted all the particulars of the shirts' failings.

"This is just unacceptable, and I ask you on behalf of us fine marathoners to please consider our proposal for better-quality shirts," he finally concluded as Lara and I looked on in wonder.

Mwaniki and Lara have a hysterical rapport and are constantly awarding each other the prize for biggest troublemaker. "Mwaniki, you *slay* me," Lara is fond of saying, while Mwaniki retorts back, "Me? I do *not* slay."

Within ten minutes of leaving the green fields surrounding Imani, we enter Nyeri town, rumored to be the fifth-largest city in the country, but which always seemed to me on par with a roaring Western town in an old movie. "So this is like the equivalent of Miami—the fifth-largest city in the country," we had told the first batch of Hope Runs volunteers who came that summer, as we toured them through the shacks on their first days in Africa and showed them where to buy their produce. A few paved streets and a few larger offices stand next to the blocks and blocks of dilapidated buildings, open-air markets, and street sellers.

An hour past Nyeri—twenty kilometers took that long on the potholed roads of the country—we arrive at the equator. Although the Imani kids have all lived their lives knowing they are an hour from the earth's mighty equator, the global impact of this for my North American sensibilities is still exciting, and I don't want to pass the equator without taking part in what I see as a thrilling science experiment.

We pull the vans over to the side of the road and pay three dollars to one of the dozen science hawkers vying for our business. With no small amount of confidence, he pours water in a jug on one side of the line and it spins right. Then he walks ten feet across the line—which says "EQUATER HERE"—and pours water into the jug again. It spins left. The children are underwhelmed, but they understand from the video camera I have in hand that this is exactly the type of nonsense mzungus like.

Mwaniki keeps talking throughout the demonstration.

"Mwaniki, stop talking so the science man can educate you," Lara tells him.

"Lara, you know me—I think this is just *so* interesting," Mwaniki goads her, rolling his eyes.

"Troublemaker," she responds.

A year later, when Mwaniki starts a profitable little rabbit hutch on the orphanage grounds using money from Hope Runs, he explains to me that one of the greatest perks of the bunny business is that the visiting white people always want to take pictures of the thriving hutch. "Mzungus love to look at bunnies," he says sagely.

Apparently, mzungus also love to watch water spin down a drain.

Several hours later we arrive in Nanyuki, a smaller town in the shadow of Mount Kenya where we are to spend the night, and Lara and I go off to pick up the race numbers and packets. "Our kids want all the gloss," we assert when a registration woman asks if we really want all the mountains of promotional materials for *each* of our eighteen runners. In the meantime, the kids busy themselves with the only tourist attraction in town—an outdoor museum featuring giant-sized Bible verses printed on the ground.

That night after we scour the town for a suitable dining venue, we eat a premarathon dinner of soda, French fries, and unidentifiable meat and then retire to our dingy hotel rooms, each one named after a different African country. As we fall asleep, Lara tells me that Joseph, twenty, said this was the first night he had spent away from the orphanage in four years.

Malawi (the room) is not good to me and Lara that night, and when we wake up at five the next morning, we have barely slept. Although getting up is miserable, staying any longer on the dirty bed we share seems even more unappealing. Pulling on our running gear (I am wearing Lara's old biker shorts and an oversized

Hope Runs T-shirt) and then piling warm clothes on top of that, we attempt to look like energetic coaches. After requisite door pounding, the teens, emerging in pairs from their particular abodes of Zimbabwe, Nigeria, and Chad, vacillate between rowdy excitement and mute anxiety. Lara and I share their feelings. We are all nervous and afraid of what's ahead.

After twenty minutes of milling around, we load into the two vans to head toward the race, and the struggling heaters do little to diminish the cold of the central highlands. I am reminded again of how distrustful I had been of the Kenyans when they told me it would get cold in June. Cold? In Africa? This obvious impossibility had left me laughing in the heat of March. Now, sitting in the front seat of the first van, passing out bananas and biscuits, I feel it.

The vans soon turn out of the main town of Nanyuki, and we drive on empty roads for an hour before turning into the Lewa Wildlife Conservancy, where the race is taking place. The Lewa Marathon is famous the world over for being the only marathon of its kind held on a game reserve. It's also considered a challenge at an altitude of nearly a mile. Dirt roads are surrounded by wild, waist-high brown brush that stretches to the horizon. Occasional acacia trees dot the landscape. The teens stare out the windows, trying to spot animals, as we all listen to Kenyan radio's Sunday morning evangelical programming.

As we come closer to the race grounds, we begin to see throngs of Africans, entire families who had been walking since the dark middle of the night to reach the race site expo in time for the start. It is a huge business day for these sellers of small goods, crafts, food, and water, and these entrepreneurs will not be missing it. The occasional African runner, decked out entirely in a Dri-Fit sports suit, jogs along the road, warming up.

"That one is very smart," Mwaniki says, admiring an outfit. And then, "Is there more biscuit?"

Having caught "Kenyan time" from the kids, we have ten minutes to spare by the time we pull into the parking lot—an appalling figure in race preparation terms. The mad dash begins to pin on numbers, go to the bathroom, and rush to the start line, where a cobbled mass of thousands stand shoulder to shoulder in aimless array. The kids are thrilled to see Catherine Ndereba, the famed Olympian world-record holder who is competing in the half marathon that day. Ndereba, it turns out, is from a village close to the orphanage. I shake my head at the small wonder of big Africa.

Everyone is clearly nervous. James, the captain, is silent; Big Rhoda, the stalwart, is more affectionate than usual; and Mwaniki is engaged in an endless banter with Lara. ("Lara, look who's here" and "Lara, look who's there" and "Lara, look at his shorts—they are TOO short" and "Lara, you are TOO funny this early morning" and "Lara, you are looking TOO tired now to run . . .") And then the runners ask Lara to pray. In an orphanage community in which every visitor who is a good person is considered Christian by default, it has never occurred to anyone that Lara might not love Jesus. To this day she is a Christian in Kenya by assumption—mostly because she always goes to church and bows her head when everyone else does. That morning she thanks God for the beautiful day.

"And Lord, please remind the Kenyans to drink water," Lara finishes.

The race begins, but given the unorganized mass at the start line, we spend the first ten minutes running on the small brush outside of the running trail. The notion of marathon pacers—individuals who run the whole race carrying signs with their expected finish times and create masses of timely followers behind them—is absent, as is any concept of starting in relation to your pace time (if you're running a three-hour marathon, you start in the front of the pack;

if you're running a five-hour one, you start in the back). Thus, we deal with the more annoying race problem of spending the first mile or two just sorting out who is really running this thing.

I never start fast, and very quickly Lara and I drift toward the back of the women's pack with some of our teenage girls nearby. Next to us plods Big Rhoda, the most dedicated of our girl runners. She's not the fastest, but she has an unending commitment to getting the job done. During the infamous *Runner's World* photo shoot strike, when many of the teens refused to run for a week after the photographer (and we) showed favoritism in photographing Sammy and Mwaniki more than the others, she had been the only secondary school girl to show up to run. She had said she would, she explained, and so she did despite the other girls' glares.

When we reach the first water station after thousands of runners have passed through, it looks typically tapped. A zebra stands awkwardly to the side of the glucose station.

"Rhoda—drink!" I bark.

"You drink!" Rhoda barks back.

As our rhythm establishes itself, so does our boredom. Those who have never run a very long race often buy into the common misconception that running a marathon is simply perpetually exhausting. For most runners, it's not. Instead, it's just boring. As I limped home on the Madrid subway with Lara after my first marathon a year and a half before, I explained this.

"You aren't tired so much as bored," I said, unsuccessfully wooing her. "And then, of course, at about the four-hour mark, you want to cut off your legs. But for the most part you never really enter a state where you feel like you need to stop for cardiovascular reasons. Your endurance can keep you going—but your legs want to kill you."

Especially for a woman who runs slowly, the massive amount of time that passes between the start line and the finish line means that you have no other choice but to somehow overcome your mind's demons through mental endurance.

At mile six, the hill begins, and the reality of the altitude gain makes it clear why they call this one of the ten hardest marathons in the world. We have a leg up, though, as we have trained on roads like this at such altitudes. During our thirteenth mile (at the end of the first loop), as we come around a curve on a small section of trail, the elite male runners who are about to win the entire 26.2-mile marathon actually pass me and Lara. Considering their marathon times are half what ours will be, it is something we should have expected, yet we can't help but laugh pityingly at our ineptitude.

Within a few months, when we hire some of these same champion Kenyan runners to coach our Hope Runs kids, one would ask Lara to give him the shoes she wore during the marathon that day. "But what size are you?" the amateur Lara asks the elite.

"It doesn't matter," he says. They were better than what he was wearing.

When we reach the same flat horizon line where we had started thirteen miles earlier, I tell Lara I am pulling ahead.

"Ever so incrementally," I add. I do this because of speed—I am infinitesimally faster than the girl running with the fever, and I also know that the only way I can make the pain in my legs go away is to finish sooner—but also because we both understand that perhaps it is important to do this part on our own.

That day everyone finishes. The downside of running the race myself is that I can't welcome the other runners across the finish line, but the video footage that Sammy takes allows me a peek into what happens before Lara and I cross the finish line.

James, the team captain, who more than once had ventured out into a dark African evening to find Lara or me struggling to bring home a lone runner who had fallen behind during our afternoon runs, does everyone proud by finishing his first marathon in excellent time. He had wanted to do better, though.

"There was a pain in my leg," he says afterward. "I missed one minute for running!"

Mwaniki and his short shorts finish with much fanfare, mostly thanks to Sammy, who documents his friend's final steps in several hundred similar photographs and video clips: Mwaniki posing with his medal against the fence. Mwaniki posing with his medal in front of a sign. Mwaniki posing with the medal lying on the grass. Mwaniki posing with a crown of flowers to congratulate himself. More than anything, though, Mwaniki loves the expo, where, true to his word, he tries to meet famous runners and women in general.

Big Rhoda is the first girl of the nine teenage girls to finish. Although her training times had not suggested she would finish first, in retrospect it makes perfect sense. In the distraction-filled world of marathons, she is the one who sticks to her dogged running plan. The zebras and glucose stations didn't turn her head—she had a race to finish, after all.

In life, I love thinking that I have been carrying the hints of my future with me all along. By the time I run the marathon at Mount Kenya that day, I have been reading about Kenya for years, becoming obsessed in a way that can only happen when one has a completely fictionalized version of reality in one's head. To have made a life materialize out of this is thrilling. As are the parts I could never have foreseen—like the running. Just two years ago I had sworn I would never run a marathon, and today here I am coaching one in a way, or at least threatening a bunch of people with homemade glucose to do one with me.

This life can throw you.

For the last twelve miles of the marathon that day, I am completely alone, passing up to twenty minutes at a time without seeing another runner. And if I don't take this fact to mean only that I am incredibly slow (I am), I can see the mighty beauty and spirituality in it all.

It is easy to make a moment out of those last twelve miles. Thinking about anything while alone in such beautiful landscape can seem powerful, and so when my mind dips into topics like the way my life has turned around and all that I have learned, it takes no effort to soon feel that the entire experience seems extraordinarily meaningful.

Inevitably, my thoughts turn to Lara and how I never could have predicted the roads we would take together. She can be maddening, of course, but she is also extraordinary and funny as heck, and it is unfathomable that I have found someone as interested in pulling off this strange life as I am. The sheer diversity of situations I have seen her in over the years has also been enough to make my head spin—a college student in a shiny tank top walking home from a frat party, a travel writer haggling over rugs in Morocco, a running coach and accidental humanitarian. Naturally, it is in Africa that I have learned to respect her most. Although our travels have highlighted our differences, the time in Africa has forced us to grow together toward one united purpose in a way that the past has never requested. It also seems to hint at good things to come.

But life doesn't end with Lara and me traveling in our twenties, and the beginnings of this reality are coming into focus. My time with Lara is preparing me for another phase in my journey. In the same way that all the travel has made me increasingly self-sufficient, the orphanage and the kids have turned me into more than myself.

Bestowing responsibility on me in a way that I don't deserve and can hardly handle, the kids have made me something new. Now, just as I have found our rhythm at the orphanage, I have learned the thing about rhythms: right when you get the hang of one, it's time to set off again.

When you are running a marathon, it is impossible to think of life as anything more than those twenty-six miles. At mile twelve, and at mile thirteen, and at mile fourteen, you become convinced that it will never actually end, and you cannot see a bridge to the next chapter. That day in Kenya, I am singularly convinced beyond all logical rationale that the marathon will last forever. Magically, though, when it doesn't last forever—and you are glowing and in pain but glowing still—you know that the high is unparalleled. And the high is why you keep coming back. This is how humanity fools us into doing things that may be hard but are really good for us—working with children, running, and doing our part.

It is the best of the world's tricks.

The next week during teatime back at the orphanage, James speaks to me about the marathon. Although he has always had one of those enviable faces whose natural resting state is one of happiness, his smile that day is broader as he gives me his simple thesis. "That day—that was such a nice day," he says. "*That* was the best day."

It is nothing new, these children hinting at their dismal pasts in brief asides, but I am overwhelmed. He is right, of course. There have been many best days in the past few years, but that one—that one topped them all. I want to tell him that a million more such days will come, but I am careful with what I say, because in the land of these children, promises are the most treacherous of things. I tell James that I agree. That was our best day.

SAMMY

CHAPTER 9

After attending the marathon, we are given a week to rest, and we do not have the regular Tuesday, Thursday, and Saturday running practices. This gives me more time to spend in school with friends and the chance to think more about what will come next for me in school.

During this period, my little cousin Xavier, the little "brother" I lived with at my aunt's house before moving to Imani, joins primary school. This means I can finally see him and my other cousin Joyce more often, and it gives us the chance to reconnect. I am still not allowed to see my sister, who has gone to live with an aunt in Nairobi, because I am told she needs to never see my brother and me to help her adjust. Because of that, I particularly like seeing my cousins.

At the time, I am not at the bottom at school, but I am also not at the top. I am still having trouble with math and am not doing well in science either. I like science, however, and have always been interested in learning facts about our world and how we came to be. In high school, we have three science classes: chemistry, biology, and physics. The chemistry teacher is wonderful, and the biology teacher is as new as we are to the high school and very enthusiastic. With a math teacher who is strict but very good, I start getting a better hold on math and all my grades start going up.

Another subject I like is Christian religious education. Since the high school is sponsored by the PCEA, this subject is mandatory. I like learning about religion, and I like connecting our work in science classes with our religious studies.

Outside of school, I take a bit of a break from running. Even though I had a great time spectating at the Lewa Marathon, I still feel annoyed I couldn't run, and so Hezron and I decide together that we aren't going to go to running practices for a while. Instead, I get more involved in Brigades.

Due to my dedication to Brigades, I am chosen to become a noncommissioned officer. This is a great thing, and it allows me to go to many camps and be on a high ranking in Brigades. We are invited to perform in many different parts of the parish, and we even perform a drill for the secretary general of the Presbyterian Church of East Africa. I love every minute of it.

I am also still heavily involved in Sunday school and the Sunday school drama competitions and singing competitions. Many secondary students stop going to Sunday school because they don't like to be seen with little kids. But I love kids and look forward to spending time with them and making them happy. The Sunday school teachers decide that I should become an actual teacher and sign me up to teach. It ends up being one of the best things that happens to me that year.

Being a Sunday school teacher comes with many responsibilities. I am supposed to make sure that the Sunday school room is clean and that all the books and Bibles and games are returned safely. I am also in charge of the keys to the room and ensuring all the students are ready for class. I love working one-on-one with the kids, and I even like the lectures I give. I also realize that being younger than most of the teachers is helping me serve as a bridge between the kids and the teachers. If a kid has a problem and is too shy to talk to a teacher, they can come to me.

The kids begin to confide in me more, and I am often approached by kids who want to talk about the hardships in their lives. Some kids talk about parents who are fighting; some talk about not having food to eat or being bullied at school. Whatever the problem, I talk and pray with them.

In this role, I begin to see more clearly the division that exists in the community between the kids with parents who live with their families and the kids like me who are orphans and live at Imani. Even though sometimes the outside kids have less than the Imani kids—no food to eat, no school uniforms to wear—they still look down on the Imani kids for not having parents and for living in the orphanage.

One day I find two young girls fighting with each other. One is from Imani and the other is an "outsider" from the village. I ask what is going on, and the Imani girl tells me she's tired of being made fun of for being from Imani. The other girls were giggling at her and whispering about her to each other. I ask the outsider why this is happening, and she tells me she is tired of being looked down on because she *doesn't* live at Imani. She explains that the Imani kids have a lot and also have each other—they can be like one big family sometimes.

This is something I haven't thought about before, and I start giving them a little lecture about how we are all equal. We may be a little well-off, we may be in a bad situation, we may be short, we may be tall—but whatever we are, we are really all the same. We are all equal. We have the same bones, and the fundamental things that make us human are in each and every one of us. I tell the girls that it doesn't matter if you're an Imani kid; it doesn't matter if you're a town kid or a countryside kid. We are all the same, just in different circumstances.

After I say a prayer, they hug each other. The next day I cannot believe my eyes when I see them sitting together, smiling. That Sunday they are sitting together again, this time laughing and cracking jokes.

A few months after I become a Sunday school teacher, I spend a Sunday learning how to cut hair. Haircutting is one of the main Sunday activities—all the kids at Imani have to keep their hair shaved to prevent bugs. I am interested in learning how to cut hair well like a barber, and I get an older boy to teach me. The first person I work on is my little friend Ephantus—the one who once got in trouble with the matrons for showering and washing his clothes at the same time. As I cut his hair, I accidentally cut his head and he starts bleeding a lot. I vow to get better!

The following Sunday is a beautiful day, and after Sunday school, church, and lunch, I immediately head out to the kinyozi—the shack outdoors where we cut hair. I am enjoying my newfound hobby of being a barber.

When I see some people giving hugs to Claire and Lara, I am confused. I don't usually see so many different people hugging them all at once, and I want to know what is going on. That's when Ephantus, who has forgiven me for cutting his head so badly the week before, breaks some really terrible news. I had known it was coming, as we had been discussing it for months ever since the marathon ended, but I am still shocked to learn that Claire and Lara are leaving the next day.

I think it is a joke until Lara approaches the haircutting shack with tears in her eyes. I still cannot believe that this news is true, so

I ask, and she confirms it—they are leaving early the next morning. I stop giving Demina his haircut, and he leaves with a half patch of hair. I see Claire coming over, and I go toward her to give her a hug. For a moment I can't see clearly, and I think, *What is happening to my eyes?* I see blurry stuff, and then I realize, of course, that my eyes are tearing up.

I give Claire a hug and hear her say she will be back. When she stops hugging me, I feel like a part of me is torn and taken away. I go to Lara, and for the first time I see Lara blowing her nose. I had seen Claire do that when she had a cold, but I realize Lara is doing it because of her tears, and I think her tears must be really bad to do that. As I give Lara a hug, I feel like the rest of the part that had remained of my heart is taken and I am left with nothing.

I had stopped spending so much of my time with Claire and Lara in the past few months after I got annoyed that I couldn't run the marathon, but to see them leave now makes me recognize how important they are and how I can't imagine being without them. It is a heartbreaking time at Imani, and I have never seen so many people crying because someone is leaving.

For me, living with Lara and Claire has been eye-opening. I have seen them sad, happy, sick, and angry. I have watched them play with the kids and help everyone with schoolwork. I have watched them run with all of us and even finish a marathon at a far-off place. And I am not the only one. Every single other person has watched as well.

When they first arrived, we weren't too welcoming. We said to each other, "We have new mzungus. Even worse, they are young!" But Claire and Lara proved to be different. They came and they were who they are, and we saw it. We saw they were being their real selves, and their real lives were here with us. Little by little, I got to know them and people got used to them. They were just like us, except they had different backgrounds and different skin.

Claire and Lara had become legends in the orphanage.

What I realize is that unlike many other white visitors who had come before, Claire and Lara had done Imani well. Instead of being visitors—different people—they became one of us; they became like sisters. It took some time, but eventually we failed to see their skin color; all we could see were the people behind the skin.

Walking on the stairs that night, I see many kids crying, comforting each other with the idea that Lara and Claire will be back. It is a grueling night for everyone. We cannot believe that the year has passed so fast. As I go to bed, I started replaying all the experiences that I had with Claire and Lara, and all our memories. I remember Claire coming in with the blonde bangs above her eyes. I remember Claire "insulting" me, and me getting mad, and I laugh at that part. I remember us talking about life and cracking jokes. I remember Lara giving me her camera, her "baby." I remember them teaching me all about computers, and I remember them confiding in me about their lives. I remember them helping me with chemistry homework. I cannot believe that just the other day they arrived, and now they are leaving.

As I am replaying all these moments in my head, someone tells me that Lara is waiting for me outside. As I walk out, I think, *I'm going to fall down, I am so sad*. I am upset, and I have no idea what to say to her.

As I give her another hug, she gives me an email address written on a slip of paper. But the email address has my name in it, not hers. She tells me that whenever I get a chance, I should write her an email. She and Claire have given the kids who most liked computers their own email addresses, and if more students want them, it will be my job to make them for other people. I tell her I will. Then she gives me the email password, which reads "ILoveClaire&Lara," and I laugh when she tells me Claire chose one she thought I could remember. I now have an email and a password and the webpage of Gmail written down all for me.

Then I give her my last goodbyes, and the matron says that she has to lock the doors for the night, so I have to go to my dorm room. I go to bed with my heart feeling heavy.

The next morning I wake up really early so I can watch Claire and Lara leave, and I see them just before they enter the car that takes them away. But the dormitory door is still locked, so I can't get out of the room to say anything more to them. I see them open the car door, and they look at the building from the top to the bottom, from the right to the left, and then they get in the car quite hesitantly. I'm not sure how they feel, but from their reactions, I can see that they have found their families here. A new part of life has come and gone for them, and I am glad to have been a part of it.

CLAIRE

CHAPTER 10

Leaving Kenya, and leaving Sammy, is one of the hardest things I have ever done.

That doesn't mean our life in an orphanage wasn't free of annoyances, of course. The water turned off reliably a few days a week. The shower always threatened to electrocute us. The children never stopped knocking on our door. But in the midst of it all, we had found a home where we felt happy, useful, and wildly loved.

My relationship with Sammy in particular was a shock. I loved all the children dearly, and there were many days when I wanted nothing more than to gather them all up in my skirts and take them with me, wherever I went next on my journey in life. But from the moment I met Sammy, I knew there was something different. Our relationship had always been distinctive, and even in an orphanage where Lara and I felt constant pressure to divide resources of attention equally among children, it had become both impossible to do so and hard to hide that we weren't doing it. Few children spent much time in our apartment (aside from the kitchen, where they ruined pots and pans making the "popcorns" and dreaded glucose concoctions alongside me). Sammy was a regular exception and could often be found on our computers doing photo and video editing.

Our commonalities were always astounding to me, and day after day I saw pieces of myself in him. His sarcastic sense of humor, his incessant drive to make a life for himself, and his ability to always think outside the box (admittedly in often crafty ways) in order to find new opportunities were things I identified with. It was with Sammy that I truly understood for the first time how parents of adopted children never feel a sense of something "missing" from the equation. Our bond was deep and strong.

One day in the weeks before we left Kenya, we were sitting in the living room of the orphanage apartment with Sammy. He had been a bit distant since the marathon—he was still angry he couldn't run, we knew—and wasn't spending all his free time with us anymore. But he still came by frequently, and we sought him out regularly to try to get him past his anger. That afternoon he was creating a video montage of some footage Lara and I had taken when we had gone on safari the month before. He was combining close shots of the lions we had seen with dramatically cheesy music, and horrific visions of bad YouTube videos to come danced in my mind. We began talking about school and what he wanted to become in life, and I felt compelled to say something bolder than I perhaps should have.

"Promise me you will work hard, Sammy, so that we can help to change your life. Because we will always be here, trying to do just that."

It was an emotional statement—for me—although I don't know if it registered for Sammy, who I imagined was a bit immune to things adults had told him over the years that never came true.

One of the challenges of living with the children was knowing that it was never your place to make grand statements about how much you cared for them or how you could help them. I knew I should never make promises to these children that I didn't know I could keep, and saying this to Sammy veered into that realm. And yet somehow I felt I could make it true. I had changed since that first lunch at Imani, the day I had looked in that orphanage mirror and asked God to keep my eyes wide open for the journey ahead. I really felt that the journey I had started that day—and the changes I had seen so far in my life—were just the beginning. Even though we would soon be leaving Imani—Lara was going back to school, I was thinking about doing the same, and we both knew we couldn't grow Hope Runs from the orphanage's ground-floor apartment—we saw our leaving as the start of the next chapter of our work with Imani, not the end.

We leave the orphanage in the early hours of a Monday morning—the children still locked inside their dorm rooms—and Lara and I barely speak during the long drive to the airport. We are exhausted, emotional, and overwhelmed by everything that has happened since we first stopped to stay that night at the orphanage all that time ago.

As the plane lifts off from Nairobi that day, I know that somehow, in a land of tiny children, I have grown up.

First comes the notion that, at Imani, I realized a greater interest in becoming responsible for someone else. I was single, yes, but I already had a desire to become a mother and had learned immensely about what that means by spending the year practicing that role with dozens of little ones. In terms of Sammy, though, this is complicated. While my parents said they were not in a position to adopt Sammy, and I know I am too close in age to pursue such a legal arrangement, the wheels in my head haven't stopped turning.

On the professional side, of course, there has also been a lot of growing up. When Lara and I began receiving recognition for our work with Hope Runs, it started to open doors, and I began to ponder the possibility of returning to graduate school for a business degree.

By the time we land back in the United States, I am decided.

I spend two months in California, running two more marathons, and then head back to Mexico, where I work for Hope Runs from afar, study for the GMAT exam for business school, and complete my business school applications. My top choice by far is Oxford University, where the Skoll Foundation has a scholarship for social entrepreneurs that provides a fully funded MBA—even living and travel expenses are included in the phenomenal package. It is, in my research, the absolute best I can find, and despite the dozen applications I turn in, the Oxford scholarship is what I'm angling for from day one.

In the wee hours of one Mexican night, I have my first interview for Oxford. Skype doesn't work, so I spend a fortune on a faulty landline. Miscalculating the time zone, I call an hour late. It is abysmal, and I am hardly hopeful for a positive outcome.

But when the email comes that I have been accepted to the program—no word yet on the scholarship—I think I have a chance at getting it. That same night in Mexico I had been searching the web and had come upon a three-week cruise of Antarctica on sale for nine hundred dollars. I had always dreamed of visiting the continent, and when the good news of Oxford comes in, I go for it. I ask my mother to go with me, and a few weeks later we board the ship. From our tiny stateroom, on a crackling phone line, I have the phone interview with Oxford that will determine my scholarship.

The ship's three-week tour ends in Buenos Aires, a place I lived for four months before Lara and I went on our around-the-world trip, and I'm eager to see the city again, so I decide to stay for two weeks in the midst of the blisteringly hot January summer.

I am in Buenos Aires when I hear that I have been granted the scholarship at Oxford, and I feel a kind of luck I have not known before. I still have nine months before the program starts and plan to spend the bulk of it in Kenya, where I hope to pass some of the time at a language school to improve my poor Swahili. By the time I make it back to Africa, however, I will find that my life has flipped again.

SAMMY

CHAPTER 11

It has been a few months since Claire and Lara left, and yet we still can't believe they are really gone, and we all expect to see them around every corner. We are still running together with a coach they found for us, and we still remember them in our prayers at fellowship.

I have returned to be a part of the running family. Practices are kept up, the coach keeps training us hard, and the team has become closer. We support and encourage each other; when one person stops trying, we help them on. I know this program has worked because we are now organizing it ourselves with the funds Claire and Lara have raised.

As a Form Two sophomore, I am starting to get more and more serious about my career and about what my future will look like. Who am I going to be? What am I going to do? I think about these questions all the time.

It is also time for me to start choosing some of my classes. I have always wanted to be a lawyer, so I choose history. I have spent years watching injustices happen to children, and I am tired of seeing kids angry, hungry, and miserable and not being able to help them.

Practicing law to assist women and children can help, I know. I am also interested in being a computer engineer, so I choose physics for that. I know that Kenya is becoming one of the leading technology hubs in East Africa, and I want to be a part of that world. It excites me to think about helping advance my country in that way.

Teaching also interests me. After being with kids in and around Sunday school, I think, *If I can have kids confide in me, if I can have kids understand me when I'm still young, what about when I get older? I could help them grow and become more intelligent.* No matter what, I know that my future career will have something to do with children. I am sick and tired of seeing kids sorrowful, and of being sorrowful myself, and I want to make sure that no other kids go through what I went through.

I become fixated on studying. And then, as my grades start going up, I start improving even more. I begin waking up earlier in the morning to study. Someone had told us that 4:00 or 5:00 a.m. is when your brain is the sharpest and it's hardest to forget things, and I find it's true. By the end of my sophomore year, I am third in my class and I cannot believe it. Ahead of me are two girls who are absolutely brilliant. And I am right behind them! I start rejoicing and thank God for giving me this opportunity to have high grades, and I ask him to help me take advantage of the knowledge my teachers are passing on to me.

Around this time, I have another friend I am close to named Grace. She joined Imani several years before, and I like how sweet and funny she is. She loves being around kids—helping them do their homework, helping them wash their clothes, giving them advice, or just doing anything.

One day as we are talking, she tells me that she would love to be a children's lawyer. I am surprised and glad that I am not the only person worried about the lives of children around us. When I ask more about her ambitions, she talks to me about many of the same things I have been thinking. In her life, as in mine, she has become sick of seeing how bad some parents treat their children. I can understand.

I start getting even more interested in children's injustices and how those who have gone through hard times as young kids have managed to come through them. I see a lot of these children around me every day, and it inspires me to know these children are able to survive like they do.

One afternoon a year later, I am coming back from school when I see a familiar person up ahead. She is white and tall with curly hair. When I come closer, I can't believe my eyes. It is Lara! Lara is back! Although we have seen Claire and Lara a few times since they stopped living with us more than a year before, it has been over six months since we last had a visit from one of them, and we are all so happy.

I think I am more excited than everyone else, however. It is Lara, my big sister! She is back!

I begin running to her and then give her the biggest hug, all the while trying to look like the "big man" that I am supposed to be, since I am in high school. She says that she is just going to be here for a short time, and she starts greeting everyone. As Kenyans do, we begin to tell her she has gotten a little rounder.

"I see you've got a little bit bigger, Lara. Nice and plump," I say with a smile.

She looks at me with the most evil eyes like she wants to devour me and says, "No, Sammy. That is not nice."

"But that is the best compliment you could ever give to a person!" I say.

She tells me, "No. No it's not."

"Yes it is!" I argue. "Skinny isn't good! The plumper, the better!"

"In America, it's considered mean," Lara tells me. "Zip it, Sammy."

Who knew? Even after living with Lara and Claire, I never knew that. We all will never fully understand cultural differences, I think.

Later Lara calls me to the orphanage apartment that she is staying in, and she starts asking me questions about everything: about school, about friends. I explain I have gotten some new friends, especially my new best friend, Simon. I tell her all about my life and about how much we miss her. I tell her that the orphanage has shut down the computer program she and Claire started for the primary and secondary school students, but the running program is going great.

Then she takes out her video camera and starts recording me, asking me about how I am doing in school and how my grades are. She begins asking really specific questions about my classes, and they seem kind of funny to me. I tell her about the science program, which is okay, and about some of the problems we are having with the lab for the chemistry classes. I tell her about my great grades in history and how much I like it. She says that she is really proud of me, and then she asks me a question that sticks with me. She asks if I would like to change schools.

I tell her, "Yes, definitely! If I could go to a better school, I would!"

In Kenya, there are district schools, provincial schools, and national schools, and their resources and prestige go in that order. My school is a district school, and it isn't good; it certainly doesn't have all the teachers or desks or supplies that it needs. However, I used to not go to school, so I am glad to be there and we do learn a lot.

As we keep recording the video, Lara tells me that Claire will watch it and that I should wave to Claire, so I go ahead and make silly faces.

That night many thoughts run through my mind. I can't understand why Lara would ask me if I want to switch schools, and I start to wonder if I could ever have the chance to go to a provincial or even a national school.

That night I study hard and do all my homework.

One Wednesday shortly after Lara leaves, when I am done with all my duties, the manager, Eunice, approaches me. She asks how I am doing, and I tell her how happy I am to have spent time with Lara. I ask a question about her Bible study group and then she says something strange: "Do you know anything about where your birth certificate might be?"

That's when I know something is definitely up. I tell her I can talk to my aunt in Nyeri, but then she says, "No, no, I'll talk to her myself."

I am so excited and start imagining what it might mean to go to a better school. A few minutes later she says something even stranger. She asks me how I would feel about living out of the country. I honestly can't believe my ears. I tell her I have only seen a plane one time in my life, but it was on the other side of a big fence and we couldn't get close to it.

I start to dream of what it might be like to go to Uganda or Tanzania for school. There was a matron at Imani who had a son who went to school in Uganda, and I thought that was the most amazing thing that could ever happen to someone. I wonder if I'd prefer Uganda or Tanzania, and then I even ask myself where I would *want* to go to school. We always watch Nigerian movies in the dining hall, so I wonder about West Africa and think how fun it would be to learn French. But then I stop wondering, because these are crazy thoughts to me.

Later that day Eunice sends my best friend Simon to tell me I need to go to her office. As I walk in, she tells me to take a seat, and I do so nervously, not knowing what is going to happen. She asks me when my birthday is, and I tell her it is December 24. All the children at Imani who don't know their birthday say it is December 24—a day before the Christmas holidays, when there is always meat to eat. This had always worked well for me.

"No, Sammy," she says. "You are wrong. It's December 23."

I am shocked. How could I have not been told my birthday was a different day? So many thoughts are running quickly through my mind at that moment. Why are we talking about my birthday? Why did Eunice talk to my aunt? What is going on? I ask her to be frank with me and tell me what is really taking place. That's when she comes clean with me. She tells me to relax and breaks the news.

She says that if all goes well, I will have the chance to finish my high school studies in the United States. There is a scholarship that Lara and Claire have found that would pay for many things, and they would pay for or fund-raise the rest. At first I am dumbfounded. I simply cannot believe what she is saying and have no idea what to make of it. There is a strange moment when I start to hear the sounds of birds and the manager's voice more clearly than I have ever heard them before. I start thinking back on my life and then thinking toward what it could be in the future. I know clearly that my life is about to change.

Eunice tells me that she will be giving me some essays I have to write, but I am too dazed to understand. I simply don't know what to make of any of this.

As soon as I leave her office, I go directly to my older brother, Muriithi, and then I call a family meeting with my cousins Wahito and Njeri. When I tell them of the development, they burst with joy. I am confused—if anyone should be joyous it should be me, but I don't feel that way. How can they all be jumping up and down if I am going to go away and leave everything behind? My family, my friends, and even my home country?

I decide that I've had enough, and I go to dinner that Friday to contemplate what I am thinking and feeling over a plate of delicious githeri, the food that always makes me think of home and of all the wonderful things here. That night the githeri doesn't taste the same. It tastes like something amazing that I have never tried before. That night at fellowship, I also feel different. I'm not the same Sammy who usually jumps up and down and runs around singing and dancing with the rest of the kids. I am a relaxed Sammy, a composed Sammy. I am absorbing everything around me and taking it all in.

That night during my prayers, I ask God to take care of me and to help us all follow through with this plan. My normally cold bed feels warm, and the hard mattress is soft. And then it hits me. My dreams. I am about to have my dreams come true. In my heart, I can't believe that I, a Kenyan orphan living in an orphanage, am about to achieve the dream of almost every Kenyan high school kid—to finish high school in the United States.

I may be sleeping in the orphanage now, but tomorrow I might have the chance to meet my hero, Barack Obama! I think.

Who am I kidding? I chuckle to myself.

And then I fall asleep.

The next morning I wake up and get ready to go out for the usual Saturday morning run. Everything about that morning is marvelous. I put on my shoes, the torn, ripped shoes I really, really love and the old shorts and sweater I have been wearing for years. Outside, it is still cloudy and the sun hasn't come out yet. With the coach, my friend and I start running. As we run, we keep going farther, and at the end of the run I realize we have completed thirty-one kilometers on just a regular Saturday.

I see that morning that you never really know how amazing something is until you lose it—or until you are about to. In my case, I am about to lose the orphanage family I have come to love. There are wonderful opportunities ahead of me, but this is a loss I will feel.

Later that morning after a breakfast of porridge, the manager calls me in and gives me the application to a high school called Maine Central Institute. I have never heard of Maine before. Is it near Alaska? That was where the missionaries Mr. and Mrs. Thomas were from, I remember.

The essay I am supposed to write is about my strengths and weaknesses as a person, and I ask some people around me to tell me what they think those might be. When I ask one friend, though, she starts getting suspicious. "Why are you asking me that?" she says. "We never talk about things like that."

Then my friend Hezron finds me writing the essay. At first he thinks it is a letter, and so he starts teasing me. "I see somebody has a girlfriend! Who are you writing to?"

Since having a girlfriend at Imani is not allowed, it is a big deal when I lie and say, "Yes, I have a girlfriend. I'll tell you about her later."

I think saying I have a girlfriend is morally worse than saying I am going to the United States, but I have doubts about telling people. I worry that they will feel jealous and will all start asking, "Why him? Why not me?"

Lara has come back for another week and is having lots of meetings with Manager and is always carrying papers around. She plays with the children and looks very busy, but I find time to tell her about my feelings. She says that, yes, she and Claire know that some kids might feel bad, so I should be sensitive to them. She explains that they had reasons for choosing me and that the manager will explain it all to the whole orphanage. She says she is happy the opportunity is for me, but she is also happy that I have earned a position fairly by doing well in school.

When I finish my essay, I turn it in to the manager, and she reads through it while I stand there waiting. I was nervous when I wrote it, and I know I said some silly things, trying to make my school sound better than it is so the school in Maine might consider me.

Manager starts to laugh very hard. "Sammy," she says kindly, "you know this is ridiculous. You have to write it again." I think she probably doesn't believe a good weakness for an application essay is the fact that I don't brush my teeth that much.

When I go to rewrite the essay, I start thinking about my little sister. Since my family had said it was better that I never see her, I have not seen her for five whole years—the entire time I have been at Imani. I start wondering if she would recognize me if she saw me. And if I leave for the United States and come back, would she recognize me then?

These questions start eating me up inside, and when I turn in the new essay I have written, I talk to Manager about them. She tells me that we will actually be seeing my little sister very soon. She says we have to go to the government offices in Nairobi in order to get a passport, then the American embassy in order to get a visa, and my sister will be nearby.

When I hear that I will see my sister, I am happier than I have felt in a very long time, and I go to my room and start sobbing. My best friend Simon comes in and sees me and teases, "Ah, big man crying." But I just let him say that, because I am so happy.

The next Monday morning, after Lara has left again, Manager comes to school and tells me that we are going to take some passport photos. After we take them, Manager takes me to lunch in a restaurant. This is the first time I have ever eaten in a restaurant, and even though I can tell it is not very nice, I try to have the highest level of etiquette.

On Friday night after fellowship, I sit with Simon on my bed reminiscing and talking about our futures. Simon is really ambitious and wants to become a successful businessman. He has lots of dreams and always talks about them. This is when I decide to tell Simon what is really happening with me and about the opportunity to go to the United States. He smiles wide and asks me, "Haven't you always told me that you would like to go study in the USA and meet that Obama you always talk about?"

I tell him I have always dreamed of that, but I never thought it was possible. He tells me I have to start thinking differently about what is possible, and I agree. "I will now try and do well and meet that Obama," I promise him.

The next morning I wake up early to find Simon curled up next to me like a little boy, and I am glad to have found such a great friend like him. I think about all my great friends that morning, and I pray to God that whenever I go to the United States I will be able to find good friends like these.

Finally, one day the manager tells me that we have all the papers ready and it is time to go to Nairobi to get the passport. After I eat my porridge, I see a car waiting for us. It is only the second time I have been in a personal car—the first time was with Claire and Lara and the *Runner's World* photographer—and I can't wait to enjoy the ride.

It takes more than three and a half hours to reach Nairobi, and when we do I am so surprised by what a huge city it is. There is a lot of traffic, and it is very hot out. Slowly but surely we get to an enormous building. When we enter, Manager begins trying to call someone on her phone. I am looking at the big buildings around me, taking it all in, when I think I see someone I recognize walk through the door. Someone I have waited five long years to see. It is my little sister, Bethi.

I can't hold back my tears and start running toward her. I pick up Bethi, who is now almost twelve, and hug her tightly. I start asking her how she is, and I realize quickly that she is so excited she is having trouble standing up. Her legs are really small and it looks like she can't walk well. My aunt, who has brought my sister here, says that she and Bethi are well, and although Bethi has some trouble in school, she is trying hard.

I want to know more about how my sister has adjusted over the years, and my aunt says that it was hard at first, but when Bethi was ten she sat down with my aunt and told her something that changed things. That day little Bethi asked my aunt what type of mother in her right mind would leave her three babies. My aunt didn't know what to say, and Bethi had simply told her, "I don't think that's my mother. You are my mother."

That moment changed my aunt's life, and Bethi's, and I am happy that Bethi found someone like her.

We must wait three weeks for my passport to be ready. It is a long process because the authorities have to make sure that, as an orphan, I am not being trafficked, and they ask me many questions about my family. The man in the suit once even asks me why I think my mother left me. I tell him I don't know and look away from his eyes.

After we get the passport, it is time to try for the visa, and I get to spend another whole day in Nairobi with my little sister at my aunt's store, where she sells lunches to workers. We walk around the park, I help Bethi with her schoolwork, and that night I sleep at my aunt's house. It is the best day.

The next morning we wake up very early and go to the embassy at 5:00. Zach, who works with Hope Runs, is my representative at the interview and accompanies me since I'm a minor. The line is long, and we sit drinking Kenyan tea. Zach brought some cheese puffs and I try one. They are a little too cheesy for me, and I don't like them very much.

The manager laughs at me. "You really are a Kenyan," she says. "But if you want to survive in America, you better start liking cheese." Zach laughs and says it is true.

Finally, after hours of waiting, my name is called. I am nervous, and I walk in repeating to myself all the questions that Zach and Manager and I have practiced in the mock interviews they made me do. Zach comes with me and sits down next to me across from the interviewer. All the interviewer wants to know is how I will be financed at school, and I explain about Claire and Lara and Hope Runs. And then he approves the visa and says to make sure we are back there in three weeks to pick it up.

I am baffled. The interview has taken less than five minutes! A few months earlier, Manager had been denied a visa to go to the United States on a trip, and here I get one in five minutes? I know that someone is looking out for me up above and that God is making things work.

Now that I have my visa approved and just three weeks more to wait, I know the time has come to start saying goodbye to my friends and family and my beloved country.

I have a big challenge in front of me to break the news to everyone at Imani. I know that some people—like Simon and Hezron and my brother and cousins—will be happy for me. But I also know that there are some who will be jealous and will wonder why I have gotten something wonderful that they didn't.

And that is what happens. When everyone finds out, and when Manager explains to everyone, most are really happy. But some are not. They say it is favoritism. I try to remind them of how, in seventh and eighth grade, some students had been chosen to go to a provincial school and no one had complained. "How is that different than me?" I try to tell them. "It's not that different. It's just this time I'm going to the US instead of to another school in Nyeri town." I do know it is a bit different, though.

Since school is closing for the year, there are many kids who don't live at Imani who I won't see again before I leave. This is hard, as these are my friends from primary school who helped me fit in when I first came to the area to live with my aunt, even when I didn't know the language and didn't have any friends.

I spend a weekend with the aunt I lived with before entering Imani so that I can say goodbye to my family. They have moved and now live in a stone house. This makes me happy for them. In turn, my aunt is happy for me and says that this visa will open many, many doors that my sixteen-year-old self cannot yet even imagine. Aunt Lydia tells me that now I have an opportunity to change my life.

"Sammy," she says, "I'm really proud of how you have proved yourself at Imani. Now this is your time to go and show the world who you are and what you are capable of. You have to go and do things that have never been done before. Help the kids from the streets. It's okay to work with people in high offices, but always remember to work with everyone in the world, not just the high-ups." She adds, "Keep smiling, because you don't know whose day you will shine up. And don't forget, make the world proud so that anyone who knows you will be honored to have known you."

Even though I have tears falling from my eyes, I keep the words deep in the bottom of my heart.

Saying goodbye to my aunt is hard. It was not always easy being with her, but this is the woman who took care of me when no one else would. When everybody in our family said no, she took in my brother and me, even though she lived in the countryside with a falling-down house made of wood that already had a dozen other people under its roof. She worked hard to make sure we had something to eat every day, and she taught us the language of the area. She helped us become people of purpose who were respected around the orphanage and in the school.

Aunt Lydia Njeri made sure we had a secure future when our mother couldn't.

To me, she is an iron-bred lady. She is a person of integrity. She is the symbol of an African woman.

Three weeks have closed in, and it is time for my goodbye. Like always, the big thing that is happening to me is happening on a Wednesday. On Wednesday morning I will drive to Nairobi to get my visa and then leave for the United States that night.

On Tuesday night the orphanage gives me a goodbye dinner. I am supposed to sit at the front of the dining hall, but I decide to sit with my tablemates as usual. That night even the people who are jealous of me are glad I am leaving, because everyone is eating meat and chapatti. It has been eight months since Christmas when we last ate chapatti with stew, and everyone is so excited. They laugh and say, "Thank you for leaving, Sammy! You are making us happy with this food!"

When Manager sees me sitting with my tablemates, she tells me I have to go to the front of the dining hall and take my seat as the guest of honor. Once again my tablemates are happy for me—one less person to share our table's portion means more food for them! On the way to my seat, I get distracted helping other kids pass out food, and Manager finds me again. She does not look happy and says sternly, "It's your goodbye dinner. Go sit down, relax." And then she tells me, "I think you're the worst guest I have ever seen." But I can tell she is not really mad, because she is shaking her head with laughter.

During that dinner, Reverend Mathu, the founder of the orphanage, is there, even though he is old now and we don't see him much. He prays for my journey and for my years in the United States, and he prays for Claire and Lara, my new guardians. A lot of people give me words of advice. They caution me about getting too involved in Western culture and tell me to be smart and know what is right for me.

After the festivities, I go to pack the few clothes I have. The matron has given me new pajamas and a big travel bag to put my clothes in. After I finish packing, the bag is still very light because I have almost nothing in it. I test it and can pick it up with my pinkie finger.

The next day we leave Imani at 9:00 a.m. Manager, Matron, my brother, and twelve of my friends all crowd into the back of the orphanage truck. Along the way, we stop a few times, and when we arrive in Nairobi we go straight to my aunt's lunch shop, where she serves us all a big lunch for free alongside the regular workers. My little sister is there, and I feel like such a proud big brother introducing her to each and every one of my friends. Then we spend a few hours roaming around Nairobi, looking at the tall skyscrapers and the handsome parliament buildings.

After our lunch we go to the embassy to pick up my visa. Everyone stays in the car while Manager and I go inside, since we don't want all seventeen people to go through the security checks.

We have been waiting only about ten minutes when my name is called. The well-dressed woman greets me and asks if I am Samuel. She looks at the passport photo to confirm, and then she tells us something we do not expect.

"There is a problem," she says gravely.

Apparently, there is something wrong with the thumbprint. They have confused the right thumb and the left thumb, and she tells us that now we'll have to wait two more weeks to resolve the issue. We explain my flight is that night, and she tells us it is impossible to do the whole process again today, but we keep pleading and pleading. She tells us to wait half an hour to see if we can fix the problem, then they take new thumbprints and we wait some more. It is the longest wait of my life.

The manager stands there, dumbfounded, not speaking, and I can tell she is praying in her head. But finally, the lady comes back with the passport and tells us that everything is good. She hands us the passport and tells me to have a nice flight. I am thrilled, and the manager gets us out of there as fast as we can to make sure we aren't called back in!

We return to the car, where everyone has been worrying for hours, and explain what happened. It feels like my trip to the United States could have been taken away any moment for such a small thing as the difference between right and left thumbs!

We head off in the truck to go to Jomo Kenyatta International Airport. During that ride, I sit with Bethi on one side and my brother on the other, holding their hands. My friends are all around me. I pray to God that I will be able to come back and see them all again one day. I know it is going to happen, but I want God to tell me for sure.

When I reach the airport, it is time to say goodbye to everyone one last time.

I start by thanking the manager. She has done so much for me over the years I have been at Imani, and everything she has done in the past few months to help me go to America has been amazing. When Claire and Lara couldn't be there, she helped with all the visa and passport applications. She has been like a caring mother, always asking if I had a coat or if I was hungry.

I say goodbye to everyone who is there—all sixteen people. I give Hezron, Simon, and my other friends big hugs, and I squeeze my brother and little sister so hard. And then it is time to walk through the place where they can't pass. Walking away is one of the hardest things I have ever done.

Soon I have lost sight of them.

SAMMY

CHAPTER 12

Walking into the airport is a goodbye to Kenya and a goodbye to my family and friends. I approach the lady from Kenya Airways to get my ticket, and she takes my bag, looking at me with a funny expression like she doesn't understand why I am carrying such a big bag with almost nothing inside. She takes my passport and then gives me two papers. One, she explains, is for the plane from Nairobi to Dubai. The next one, she says, is from Dubai to New York. She staples them together and puts them in my passport.

Then she looks at me again and says very carefully, "Do not lose that passport or the two papers." I remember Manager telling me exactly the same thing.

After I pass through the airport's security, I go into an internet café. I log into the Gmail account that Claire and Lara set up for me and send them an email saying I am in the airport and can't wait to see them. I log off, and the man tells me it costs two dollars. I can't understand that, since I was only on for one minute!

I find the gate where the plane is waiting. A lady at the gate asks me for my boarding passes, and I look at her, confused. Then she says she'd like to see my passport, and inside she finds the two papers. "These are the boarding passes," she explains. She takes the passes, puts them on a scanner, and lets me go inside the plane. I go on the ramp and into the plane, and I simply cannot believe that I am here inside a real plane.

It is huge. It has four seats across and is so much bigger than a car. I sit down, and as soon as I do I fall asleep. When I awake, the plane is on the ground and I think we haven't left yet. But then I look around and can sense that something is different, and I realize I have arrived in Dubai. I slept through the first flight of my life!

My boarding pass tells me to go to Gate 52, but I have no idea how to get there. I decide to ask around, but everyone looks so busy. I find a man cleaning the floor, a janitor, and he gives me directions. I realize I want to call Claire and Lara to tell them I am in Dubai, so I ask the janitor how I can do that. He says I need to buy a calling card to make the call, so I do. It costs me twenty-four dollars, almost the rest of the thirty-five dollars I started with in Nairobi. I call the cell phone, but no one answers, so I leave a message. After the call, I don't know what to do with the card. So I decide to give it to the janitor, and he smiles from ear to ear. I wonder if I have seen a smile bigger than that before.

I am running out of time, so I race to the gate but get lost along the way. The airport areas all look the same. I return to where I found the janitor originally, and he is still there. I explain I can't find the gate and ask if he doesn't mind taking me. He guides me straight there, and I see that people all around me are getting on. I board the plane and am shocked all over again that it is so much bigger than the Kenya Airways plane—it has ten whole seats running across! I am amazed and do some calculations to realize there must be almost four hundred people on the plane. I am baffled at how a plane can be as big as this, and I don't understand how it can stay in the air for more than a few minutes.

I sit in my seat and find myself next to a nice man named Joost from Canada. He tells me he is a university professor, and I think he is the coolest guy I have ever met. I am happy to have made a new friend.

Soon it is time for the plane to take off, and I start to have doubts again. How can a plane this big fly in the air without falling? I remember the things Claire and Lara had written in a long letter about the plane ride—how it will feel and what it means when it starts shaking at first—but it doesn't help much. When we get into the air, we start going up and up, and I decide to look out the window. It is amazing to see how many lights are on in Dubai. I never thought in my life I would see such a thing as that city from high in the air.

When we have been in the air for about five minutes, I am still holding my arms tightly to the chair as if the plane will fall. Within a few minutes, I decide if everyone else thinks it is okay, I will also be okay. My fears slowly go away.

We have a delicious dinner, but I don't want the cheese, so I put it aside to give to Claire. Then I fall asleep. When I wake up, we are above a body of water, and I can't believe how huge and immense the blue is. I get a little scared again, so I start a conversation with Joost to distract myself.

As we chat, the flight attendants come by, passing out drinks. When they come past me, I say I only want water, but then I see that they are giving things to people for free. I want some soda, because I have never had things like that for free before, so I point to what I want. But when I open it up and take a sip, I am disgusted. The flight lady gave me beer!

I hate the very feeling of beer on my tongue. In Kenya, drinking is looked down upon, and the only people who drink are the drunkards who live in the streets and beat their wives.

Joost, who sees me take a sip of the beer, says, "Oh! So you drink!" And then he says, "Cheers!"

I say, "Cheers!" also, and I think that sounds funny. But the beer makes me feel disgusting, so I put it down. Then I start explaining things to Joost, saying, "Well, you see . . . when I'm flying I don't like to drink beer. That way if something bad happens to the plane, I won't be drunk." It doesn't make much sense, but I just don't want to look different, so I keep talking.

By and by, I fall asleep again, and eventually we arrive at a huge airport called JFK, where we ride around on the plane for twenty minutes before it is time to get off it. As we are leaving, I decide to follow Joost, so I make sure he is right in front of me. We walk past the front of the plane, where the seats are even bigger, and he gives me a bag full of stuff that he says people who pay more to be on the plane get for free. I am excited.

When I step out of the plane with my bag of free things, I realize I am in America. I know then that my life has changed and taken another turn. I know I'll never be the same Sammy again.

Joost takes me to another security checkpoint and tells me he will be waiting on the other side. I know Joost is hurrying to catch his own plane, but he waits for me at all the security checkpoints and helps me get my bag.

Finally, we get to the checking area for my Boston plane. The lady takes my passport and enters my name in her computer, but then she has a confused look on her face. She can't find my name in the computer. Joost takes out his phone and we reach Lara. She talks to me, and then they talk for a few minutes before Lara also talks to the airline lady. I can hear Lara over the phone trying to explain everything, but she is also confused about what has happened. Apparently an airline representative was supposed to meet me between flights, and Joost was clearly not an airline representative.

Suddenly, a bell rings in my head, and I remember that Claire might have used the Kenyan way of referring to people—my second name, Ikua—when she booked the ticket. So I ask them to look for Sammy Ikua, and ta-da! My name shows up.

I ask the lady to put that name on my ticket, and she prints it out and gives it to me. Joost then starts running away, saying he has to catch his plane, so I am left shouting my thank-yous and goodbyes to him. Luckily, he has given me his phone number and his email address. I will email Joost later that day once I've arrived in Boston. His help was the best welcome to the United States I could have imagined.

While I wait to get on the last plane, I make another friend. Her name is Robin, and like Joost, she is interested in me. She actually wants to take pictures with me, and when I ask why, she says she wants a picture with the future president of Kenya!

I sleep the whole way to Boston, and when we arrive, I go to get my bag. Then I see Lara standing there with a big sign that says, "Welcome to America, Sammy." And I could not be happier.

Lara's mom, whom I had met in Kenya, is there also, and after we hug we walk outside. The summer air in Boston is so heavy that I can't breathe. We drive for a while and then arrive at a very nice house in a quiet area with lots of green grass, and I get into a bed that Lara says was her bed when she was growing up. One minute later I am asleep.

The next morning when I wake up, the air is fresh, and out the window everything looks so beautiful and green. I can see trees— lots of them—and I know I am in a totally different place. But I feel strange because the room looks so nice. The curtains are white and the bed is so pretty. And it is all so clean.

And then I look on the floor.

I see it is filled with pieces of little glass. That gives me a shock, and I don't know what is happening. And then I see a post on the floor, and a broken bulb, and I immediately realize I somehow tipped over a light and broke the light bulb while I was sleeping.

I open the door carefully to go apologize to Lara. I feel so scared and don't know what she is going to say. But instead of Lara, I see Claire, who greets me with a huge hug and looks so excited to see me. But I am not very happy, as this is one more person to know that I messed up Lara's house on my very first day.

I go to Lara to bid her good morning and to apologize for breaking the glass. But when I start apologizing, she laughs and says, "No worries!" She tells me that she heard the bulb break during the night and that it is easy to clean up. She makes fun of me that I could sleep through such a noise. It is the first of many, many times Lara and Claire will marvel at my ability to sleep through anything. With her teasing, I know it is okay, and then my heart is at rest.

They serve me a really delicious breakfast. I haven't eaten in a long time, and I have never in my life had cereal, so I eat a lot. After the wonderful food, I go to take a shower. Lara gives me a towel and shows me the shower, and the sink to brush my teeth, and the toilet. I have never seen a toilet bowl before like this and am amazed how nice it looks. It is nothing like a pit latrine, and nothing smells badly and there are no bugs.

It is the first time in my life taking a shower in hot water and without a bucket, and I shower for more than an hour. The soap smells so good. I spend forever in that bathroom, and it is one of those moments I'll never forget.

Then I put on my best clothes, as I am told that we are going to go out. We walk out of the house and go toward a car, but I am not sure who is going to drive. What I don't know is that Lara and Claire can drive, and this comes as a big surprise. In Kenya, not many people can drive, so everyone uses drivers. When Lara starts driving, we head out on some really nice, smooth roads. This is so different from the drive I'd taken from Nyeri to Nairobi just days before! Here there are no bumps at all, and it feels nothing like the two times I have been in cars in Kenya.

Lara and Claire are excited, and we start talking about everything all at once. They tell me we have one weekend to explain everything about America, as I am already supposed to be at school. The delays with the visas and passports mean that I have less time to prepare than they planned. So they just do not stop talking.

One of the first things we talk about is the cost of things in America. They say they want to teach me to understand money and how much things cost. Like how much a piece of pizza or a dinner costs, for example. If I want candy or ice cream, I need to have an understanding of the American dollar. We even talk about the costs of houses and cars—I can't believe that a house costs more than a car, as that is backwards to life in my village. I realize quickly that the American dollar isn't worth nearly as much in the United States as it is in Kenya.

One of the first places we drive to is a mall in Boston, where I am amazed by all the elegant shops. There are so many different food places and clothing stores, and it is all such a new world for me. While we are in the mall, I see a car in the middle of the building, and I am so confused. People are signing up for a contest to win the car. But I am trying to understand how a car can get into the middle of the building. Was it built in there?

I have pizza for the first time, and it is one of the most delicious foods I have ever eaten. I think about how wrong I have been about cheese. I still have the cheese I saved from the plane to give to Claire, and I remember to give it to her later. We talk a lot about race, and Claire and Lara explain that race relations are very different in the United States than in Kenya. I keep feeling stunned that not everyone around me is black. For my whole life, everyone around me except for Claire and Lara and a few others has been black. And now only some of them are. Claire tells me that when we go to Maine, there will be a lot less black people than in Boston, and that confuses me. *Less than here?* I think, shaking my head. I don't know how that is possible.

It is a long day of learning about everything very fast, and then we go home to Lara's parents' house and have a delicious dinner. I am happy to find orange juice, as it was one of my favorite things in Kenya, but in the United States it isn't very sweet, so I do not like it. I realize that like everything else, orange juice is different in the United States and Kenya.

We spend the next day, Saturday, sorting out all the clothes Claire and Lara have collected for me to cope with the weather in Maine, where my scholarship is. I don't know why I need all these different clothes, but they just keep telling me I can't understand how cold it is there. Whenever I say I am used to the cold in the Kenyan Highlands, they shake their heads and say, "It's a little different than that."

On Sunday Claire has to leave. I know she has a new job and can't go to all these places like Kenya and Maine with Lara, and she says how sorry she is. But I am not sure why she is so sorry. I feel lucky she was in Boston with us.

On Monday morning, bright and early, we are on our way to school. I think three days is probably the shortest time in the history of the world that anyone has ever immersed himself in a new culture!

Lara and I pack the big bag I now have and put it in the car, and then she says she is going to drive all the way to Maine. She says she thinks it will take about four hours, so if I want to sleep in the car I can go ahead and do so. I am glad about this, because I am so tired from all we have done over the weekend.

As soon as we pull out of Boston, I fall asleep. When I wake up, I see one straight road ahead with many trees on one side, and she tells me we are in a state called New Hampshire. I start wondering why there is no one around. There are no people or houses on the side of the road, only cars coming and going in both directions.

Then she explains that we are on an interstate, a state highway. She says that in America the state highways don't have people on the side of them, because people think it is dangerous. Then we start talking about more cultural differences that we haven't discussed yet.

One example, she says, is drinking wine. She explains how she knows that in Kenya, drinking alcohol is really looked down upon. But in the United States, she says, many people over the age of twenty-one have drinks sometimes. (She makes it clear that I cannot drink!) It might be a glass of wine, it might just be something small. But people do drink—even good people and even good Christians. She says she and Claire have wine sometimes at dinner. She explains that many of the rules from Kenya are different here, and I need to be careful what I assume about people I meet. But she also tells me I am a good kid and that I should trust my feelings and my intuition and always ask her or Claire if something seems wrong.

We also talk a lot about consequences—that I will see kids doing things I know are wrong and I might be tempted to join them. She explains that though I am still a kid I also need to act like an adult—I have a great opportunity, and I need to be mature enough to remember that and to act more responsibly than other children my age.

Sooner or later we see a sign that says, "Welcome to Maine." She sticks her foot out toward the front window of the car, and she says she entered Maine first!

With Lara's teasing words, I understand this new place will become my home. My state of mind begins to change drastically. I start getting excited, thinking about my life and wondering, *Really, what am I doing here?*

About two hours later we enter Pittsfield, where my school is. This time I am the one to stick my foot toward the front window of the car and say, "I entered Pittsfield first!" Lara looks happy that I am so excited.

When we arrive at the school, Maine Central Institute, or MCI, we meet up with a man named Mr. Clint Williams, who has helped Claire and Lara get the scholarship for me. He starts showing us around the school, and it is so large and beautiful I am sure it is really a university. I thank him for the wonderful opportunity, and then he walks me to the registrar, where he says I have to go see my class advisor to be able to pick my classes and take my English and math tests.

As we talk with the advisor, he explains to me about the extracurricular opportunities at MCI. He is also the head coach of the soccer team, and when he asks if I want to play soccer, I say, "That's a really good idea. I'd love to do soccer."

Lara jumps in and suggests, "If there is cross-country or track, he's been doing cross-country!" I try to picture doing the same running in this new place that I had always done in Kenya, and I cannot imagine it.

After I take my math test, the teacher places me in an advanced math class, and after the easy ESL test, they place me in a normal English class. Then we start talking to the nurse so I can be cleared to live in the dormitories. She explains that I need a few more vaccines. This comes as a shock, because we did all the vaccines we thought we needed in Kenya. Apparently, though, it wasn't enough, so it is back to the doctor's.

For two nights, Clint Williams lets us stay with him while everything is finished up. Mr. Williams has two small children, and Lara uses the time to teach me to ride a bike. Even though I am scared,

I do it. Lara says I learn fast, and I am thrilled with the feeling of the bike.

On Wednesday—always a Wednesday in my life—it is time for classes to start.

At lunch that first day I am introduced to the new cross-country coach, who says she is really glad to have a Kenyan on her new team. She tells me it is the first year they have had a cross-country team, and she is excited. So am I.

Joining cross-country gives me a whole new routine. I wake in the morning for breakfast at 7:00. Breakfast is always really good, and I am amazed to have eggs every single morning. Homeroom starts at 7:45, lunch is at 11:45, and then we leave school at 3:00 p.m. After school, I go straight to cross-country practice. Dinner is at 5:00, and then we have study hall and lights out at 10:30.

For the rest of my time at Maine Central Institute, this will be my routine, and the time begins to fly by quicker than I expected. I work hard in my classes to get good grades. Math proves easiest for me, and I progress quickly. Even in English, my third language, I do better than the average student, and I am proud of myself.

Most challenging of all, though, is the number of general references in school to American things I don't understand. For example, a teacher might name a musician or talk about something that once happened in the United States that I have never heard of, and I get really confused. Although I love my history class and have one of my favorite teachers (who is also my track coach), this problem with references happens constantly! It seems Americans and Kenyans learn very different history lessons. When they say "the civil war," I am thinking of something very different.

It is in my biology class that I have to do a research project, a two-page report on mammals. It is my very first research paper in my whole life, so I go to the library and get on a computer and google "mammals." I haven't spent much time in my life on the internet, except for when Claire and Lara taught a computer class at Imani, and I see that it has everything. On the very first page that comes up, I click on a page that looks good. It is called Wikipedia.com.

As I read the information on the page, I think it is really interesting and certainly very full of information. Some of the information I know and some of it I don't, and this makes me know that it is perfect for my research assignment. So I copy the page, open up a Word program, and paste the text right into it. I put my name, Samuel Gachagua, at the top, and write a title: "Research on Mammals." I think it is the best thing I have ever done in my life—my very first research paper! I am really excited.

The library lady helps me print out the paper, and I turn it in. The next day in biology class, Miss Cardenas, who is also my cross-country coach, comes to me with my paper and tells me that she has given me a 60, which is the lowest grade possible. She calmly explains that I cannot copy and paste things from the internet. This is a new concept to me, and it takes me time to learn the differences between cheating and researching. (Now I look back on that paper and laugh at how wrong it must have seemed to my teachers, but it took a long time for me to learn this important lesson. At the orphanage, we copied from each other's papers all the time, and no one noticed or taught us it was wrong.)

The next research project I have to do is a joint project on the bayou. I am still intimidated by white students, as they seem to know everything and I am sure they are much smarter than I can ever be. I am convinced that my friend Forrest is disappointed by the fact that he has been assigned to do a project with a clueless African counterpart who has no idea what the bayou is.

I decide to seek help on the project after school at the library, and I ask the librarian a lot of things to help me better understand computers, websites, and the internet. I spend about three days in the library getting help for my research on the project, and after all the research it is time to start typing up the project with For-rest. He tells me that because he has done more of the research, it is my job to type the three-page paper. He doesn't know what he is getting into, though.

I say, "Okay!" and start typing.

As he watches, I can see his frustration growing by the minute. I don't know what he is getting so worked up about until he shouts at me, "You type too slow! Give me the darned computer!"

As he types, I am quite simply stunned. He isn't looking at the keyboard but at the monitor, and he is typing really, really fast. And then I realize that he must have been going crazy watching me try to type. I reason, though, that it isn't my fault. It is the fault of the person who made the keyboard the way it is, because since it is not in alphabetical order it is impossible to find the keys quickly. I just don't understand why someone would do that.

To solve the problem, I decide to go back to the library and take some typing lessons from the librarian. She installs a program in one of the computers where I just type the words that are shown on the screen. Slowly I improve, and I eventually type the conclusion for our project. It takes me two days, and I work hard on it. Although we don't get the best grade on the project, I am really proud of how I have learned to deal with the issues that come up, and I know I am getting better. Progress is slow, but it is happening.

At MCI, I become very involved in extracurricular activities, and they are an important part of my experience in high school. I hold various leadership positions in the diversity club, the resi-dential student council, and others. It seems all my activities in Kenya carry over to the United States and somehow become more official. Like the singing and drama I did in church, acting with the drama club lets me join a group to put on a production. I start by working on the sets but then take acting classes and join a lot of plays. Early on, this helps me to integrate better into American culture and the American high school scene. I make new friends, and others start to see me not as the "naïve African student" but instead as Sammy—not a skin color but a person.

I join a lot of groups, but sports come to really define my years at MCI. It starts with cross-country, where Miss Cardenas inspires me from the beginning and helps me to integrate with other students. Whenever I have problems or questions, I go to her and ask her questions. By training with her in cross-country and learning from her in biology, I get to know her well, and she becomes one of my greatest mentors in school.

When I start cross-country, I am horrible at first. I am surprised by this because I am Kenyan and I have run for years with Hope Runs, but these students are all so fast. I see that when we were running in Kenya—with Claire and Lara trying as coaches—we were not really training as seriously as I thought we were. The idea of training was so new that I thought we had a rigorous schedule, and it was amazing to watch what we accomplished over the many months of running. I realize now at MCI why Claire and Lara were always pushing us harder and telling us we could do more. At the orphanage we were dedicated, but we were not experts.

But I do not get discouraged. I have seen that with running, the more you work, the more you improve. So I keep practicing, and slowly I become one of the fastest on the team.

However, it is cross-country that finally gets me in the hospital for the first time in my life. I am at a championship run during my senior year, and it is cold and rainy. I am very hopeful that day because it is going to be one of my last races as a cross-country runner in high school, and I want to do the best I can and get a good position. After about five minutes of running, though, my head starts spinning. I don't know what is happening, but I keep going. I can't see very far, and the distance I can see clearly keeps shrinking. A terrible headache starts growing stronger and stronger, and I am getting dizzier and dizzier. I should stop but I don't. Instead, I just let the guy behind pass me, and I follow him, not able to see the path clearly. I keep running, and all I can see is haziness.

When I pass the finish line, I can hear people saying, "Keep walking, keep walking." And so I keep walking until I don't remember anything else.

What I do remember is waking up on the ground and realizing that Coach Cardenas is there asking me, "Are you okay, Sammy?" She tells me I have been lying there for five minutes, but I have no idea why. It sounds like she is speaking a really weird language, and then she picks me up, but as soon as she does I lose consciousness again.

The next time I wake up, I am in an ambulance, and it is going as fast as possible, it seems to me. I am getting really scared. All I can see is Coach Cardenas right next to me, and Megan, my friend and fellow captain, is there too. We go straight to the hospital, but the whole way I am so confused and talking about weird things.

As soon as I get to the hospital about twenty minutes later, the school president and some other people are already there and ask how I feel. I am better, and the dizziness is almost gone.

Over the course of days and days, they do many tests to find out what happened to me. In the end, the doctor tells me that I have a blood condition called alpha-thalassemia, which means I have little red blood cells that are shaped like rice instead of being hollow disks like they should be. The doctor explains that for me personally, this may have been a good thing, as I had a smaller chance of getting malaria back in Kenya. However, the condition can cause problems, as it had on the day of my race, and I would need to be careful. It also means that if I marry a spouse with the same problem, our little baby might not grow past a young age. I find it funny to think of having babies, but I realize that like most things, my health has good and bad parts. It was awesome not to get malaria, but there is still a consequence for my life.

Over the years there would be many more trips to the hospital and a lot more health questions that needed to be answered. Growing up as I did, I have realized there are long-term health consequences and we can't know much about my health background, so a lot of tests and doctors would become part of my next few years, thankfully without anything too serious.

I recover from the race and am able to return to practice. I love cross-country, and my success boosts my relationships with friends around school and my well-being in general. By the time I have finished three years of running, I have been named one of the best runners in the region, earning a sixth-place position. Becoming a cross-country captain is something I had really been hoping for, and when I become a senior, the coach tells me I have proven myself, and she makes me a captain.

Track and field also becomes something I am very proud of. I had practiced more at long-distance running in Kenya, so in my first year of track and field I am not able to qualify for any championships. I volunteer myself to the coach to join the race-walking program, which at first he discourages. I convince him to let me try—I just believe that all my years of walking were the perfect training—and I not only make the team but also eventually become a state champion.

Outside of running practice, I find a way to help MCI's teams like I helped Lara and Claire with the marathon when I couldn't run. I become involved with the postgraduate (PG) basketball program at MCI as their manager. As I did with the Lewa Marathon, I travel with the team and help get everything ready and even help with photographs. The boys who play PG basketball are older and tougher, and some are even black like me. We become friends in a way, and I follow their team to the New England championships.

My world at MCI becomes very busy and very full. I love my activities but am exhausted trying to keep up with everything, with Lara and Claire always pushing me to keep my grades up. They talk about my future and college and urge me to try really hard.

However, being in the United States isn't just about school; it is also about family. Over the years Claire and Lara and I become much closer, and I get to know their friends and their extended families.

CLAIRE

CHAPTER 13

Buenos Aires is not a new city to me. Several years before, in the months before my trip around the world with Lara, I had lived in the large metropolis. Absurdly, making Buenos Aires my home was a fantasy born out of a love for an Argentine soap opera about singing orphans that I became addicted to while living in Mexico. I love the Argentine city of steak and wine and tango, and my mother and I rent an apartment to stay in the city for two weeks after the cruise, before I head back to Africa. A few days before my flight is set to leave, a distant friend from college who is spending a year in Buenos Aires invites me to come to dinner with some of her friends.

"I want you to meet someone in particular," she says. "He's the perfect international man." And she emails me the picture of an incredibly handsome Argentine playing a guitar.

I am seated at the Italian restaurant in a black and white sweater vest with a handful of people around me when José walks in, and from the moment he sits down at the head of the table, I am certain

I can fall in love with this man. Partway through the dinner, people move seats so we can sit next to each other—it is something of a setup, after all—and we begin talking. To this day we do not remember in what language we spoke.

I am nervous, tearing at the label on my bottle of water, when I mention that I once rented a car and drove to the hotel that is the inspiration for the logo on the water bottle, a place in the far western Andes in Argentina. He knows it and nods. "It's just like the hotel in that old movie *The Shining*," he says. "Abandoned and amazing."

He had been there too.

When I had gone there, I thought that very thing and wanted to stay at the place for days, intrigued and scared all at once. I want to say so now but assume this strange man from another land will think I am out of my mind. So instead I smile wide.

The strange kinship over the creepy movie, and the fact that I ask bold, wildly inappropriate questions for a first meeting—"Why aren't you married? How did your last relationship end?"—make José pause. By the end of the night, he has come to two conclusions.

One, I am a bit dark. And two, he is intrigued. He asks me to go for a bike ride the following weekend—is he asking me on a date? I can't tell, but either way, the next morning I call the airline and change my flight so that I can stay in Argentina an extra month.

I stay for nine, and I marry José.

I am bumping along a horrid African road in the bush with Lara a few months after that Italian dinner in Buenos Aires. It is my second trip to Africa since leaving the orphanage the year before, and my first with Lara. It feels like old times, except that things are different now. Hope Runs has grown dramatically, and we have much more on our plates in running the nonprofit.

When I tell her I am in love with José, she says, blindsided as I was, "I really didn't see that one coming."

Life has thrown me.

After nine months in Argentina—with several trips to Africa sprinkled in between—I begin business school in England. At Oxford, I wear layers and shiver out the year, wondering why no one has ever explained to me that darkness envelops England at 4:00 p.m. for so much of the year. José visits several times, and we freeze and drink tea together and talk about our future, which now involves too many continents to count, it seems.

In Oxford in the fall of 2008, I meet Biz Stone, the cofounder of Twitter, a tiny startup of a dozen employees, and get an offer to join the company to help others use the platform to do good in the world.

It was at Imani that I had learned to use Twitter, after all. Many a night you could find me wildly waving my cell phone above my head on the roof of the orphanage, trying to catch a spare cell phone bar. After connecting my Bluetooth dongle to my cruddy red dirt–encrusted cell phone, I tweeted about what it was like to "coach" kids who sprinted faster and farther than I ever could, and about running in the mud with eight-year-old girls in discarded prom dresses holding my hands. Overwhelmingly, I tweeted about a far-off life, trying to fumble toward doing good by doing well.

The tiny company had taken notice, publishing a post on the Twitter blog in 2006 about my joining the platform and some of the tweets I had sent (on some days, it could take thirty minutes for one to upload).

And then everything happens at once.

Just as work is starting with Twitter in San Francisco and José and I are planning our future together, we find a way to bring Sammy to the United States.

When my parents had declined to adopt Sammy the year before—my father joking years later that he couldn't possibly face another four years with my younger brother's miserable track coach at Berkeley High School—we started looking for other paths. Sammy was still a minor, and I was too close in age to adopt him.

We are at our college friend's wedding in Boston in the spring of 2009 when Lara pulls me away from my assigned seat at the reception dinner. We are seated at separate tables, and as the make-your-own wedding sundaes come out, she grabs me, hissing, "I'm sitting next to someone you want to meet."

By chance, she had been placed next to the financial aid director for a boarding school in a small town in Maine. "We're always looking for interesting international students," Clint Williams explained.

We jump into action.

By the end of the dinner, we are wild with the idea.

The logistics, though, prove one of the biggest headaches we could ever imagine. The timeline, for one, is bad. We have four months before his sophomore year in Maine would start, and four months is not a long period of time to move the mountains that need to be moved. There are endless problems to be dealt with, and had we a hint that night of what we would have to go through, I'm not certain we ever could've convinced Maine Central Institute to take on such a challenge.

Some things prove easier than others. The orphanage has no qualms and agrees with us that it is a great idea and we should do everything we can to pursue it. Sammy, on his end, is thrilled, and the orphanage manager, Eunice, is immediately willing to do whatever she can to make it happen. That said, communication with the orphanage is always difficult, and when we try to move quickly on a big project, it proves expectedly challenging. Since we left, they've returned to having almost no internet access whatsoever, so the only way to communicate is to call Eunice and hope that the rural Kenyan reception is in our favor. The only way we can talk directly to Sammy is by calling Eunice and having her put Sammy on the phone if he's not in school.

Quickly it becomes clear that we can't manage things from afar, but the timing for me falls between the last months of business school and the first months of my new job at Twitter, a small start-up more fast-paced than I could have ever dreamed. Lara takes everything on and makes two trips during the late spring and summer to deal with some of the unending issues: finding Sammy's birth certificate, getting Sammy a passport (since he's an orphan, this is hugely difficult), getting his vaccinations, and ultimately getting him the visa to come. Amazingly, he doesn't get his visa in hand until hours before his flight to the United States.

The day he leaves Kenya, I am sick with worry. We have sent him a seven-page letter outlining exactly what will happen on the plane in order to ease his fears, saying, "As it starts to move, it will shake a lot and it will feel scary, and then it will get louder and then start going faster and faster. The shaking will increase, but you do NOT have to worry. It ALWAYS does this and this is PERFECTLY NORMAL." This is the child, after all, who saw his first elevator and water fountain in the American Embassy when doing his visa interview a few weeks before.

My worries abate, however, when we receive an absurd phone message from him in Dubai, in which he says he just wanted to "see what's up!" and spends most of the time talking about the nice men he has met in the Dubai airport. It is beyond anticlimactic but truly hilarious. No mention of a scary plane flight, no mention of culture shock or fear. Just a teenage boy spending a fortune to call us and ramble on.

My father, after hearing this, tells me, "It sounds like Sammy's going to do just fine here."

I take a red-eye after work from San Francisco on Thursday night, and it kills me that my flight doesn't arrive until the morning after Sammy gets in. When I see him Friday morning, sleepy and overwhelmed and mumbling about a lamp he knocked over, I cannot believe he is really here. There were so many times in those months of stress when I had resigned myself to realizing that the challenges were insurmountable and that this dream was not going to come to fruition. And yet it has.

That weekend is a whirlwind.

The first morning, in the car to start the round of endless chores, we talk to him about prices. What things cost in America, what salaries people make, and how those costs relate to the weekly allowance we'll be giving him at school. Translating numbers into shillings makes him even more baffled. What he once thought was a fortune in American dollars has now been reduced to the cost of a slice of pizza in this foreign place.

One night we go to Harvard Square and eat takeout vegan food with Lara's family and buy large Starbucks iced coffees (Sammy puts in six sugars), which he tells us he immediately loves. Coffee becomes a staple for him in Maine.

He brings a large suitcase with him that is nearly empty, and when we open it we find a motley collection of tragically unsuitable clothing items. Sammy says the orphanage matrons had taken him to the storeroom and given him "new" (newly donated) clothes. I pull the items out one at a time—too-small plaid pajamas, a chartreuse green blazer, dress pants five sizes too big—and marvel at how out of place they look in Lara's parents' home, here in Boston amidst our excess. None of them will do, we know.

We go to Marshall's to buy any remaining clothes he needs that we didn't already collect from friends and family, and he loves everything. Every time I give him a new polo to try on, explaining the dress code at Maine Central Institute, he dances and wiggles his hips.

Quickly Lara and I fall into a rhythm of this bizarre form of long-distance parenting we have gotten ourselves into. Relying on the incredible staff and teachers at Maine Central Institute, we bumble our way through the school years.

Parenting from afar is a challenge that never goes away, and we come to lean heavily on people who see Sammy on a daily basis—his teachers and resident advisors—in ways that other parents surely don't need to. In Sammy's first years, he is paired with two guardian angels—Mrs. Pomeroy, a young, new resident advisor at the school, and Declan Galvin, a young teacher who recently graduated college and returned to MCI, where he himself went to high school. Mr. Galvin—it takes us years to call him Declan—studied in Kenya during college and speaks good Swahili. He is a godsend, and he will stay in Sammy's life long after MCI and save him time and time again.

I quickly find that one of the hardest elements of our parenting is the nature of discipline and consequence setting. I have not had the luxury of raising Sammy with my values during his formative years, nor am I able to live with him on a daily basis for nine months of the year, and both of these issues cause problems. The hardest challenge, I find, is how to effectively discipline him when he makes poor choices in order to teach him to do better next time.

I read a number of books on the topic but come up dry again and again. Shockingly, most are not written for twenty-something women trying to parent teenage orphans. My father is able to describe the situation best when he says that Sammy's life—in Sammy's mind—likely feels like one big roll of the dice. The good things and the bad things that have happened to him in life have seemed to him entirely random and outside of his ability to control, predict, or plan for. Thus, he is able to live in the present to an extent that we simply cannot understand.

I grew up believing that if I set goals for myself or behaved a certain way at home or at school, my efforts would be ultimately rewarded with positive things: a good relationship with my family, getting into a good college, a good job, a good life at large. There might be hiccups, but for the most part I could work hard and be rewarded.

For Sammy, none of this has been true. First he was born into a tragic childhood. Then he won a golden ticket and entered a wonderful orphanage. Then he received an abundance of riches when he was given the chance to study in the United States. But why?

Sammy believes fervently in God, but it is hard to reconcile God with the path of his life. Why did God give him a father who died and a mother who abandoned him? And why did God choose *him* to be the lucky one to enter Imani, when so many other children in his community did not have that opportunity? And then why did God go further and give him a way to come to the United States? We talk about this again and again. The answers, I always say, are harder than I know.

Unfortunately, the nature of his life circumstances means that for him, psychologically, there is a lack of long-range goal setting with an eye toward achievement. On a deep level, Lara and I come to understand, he seems unable to understand the true consequences of not giving his all in a class he doesn't care about, for example, because on some level he believes success for him really is random, after all.

Sammy lives in the moment in a way I've never seen. But the very characteristic that has allowed him to reinvent himself time and time again and be resilient in the face of horror has also brought clear downsides. He is forgetful to a fault, he has trouble planning for the future, and only by our diligence is he able to meet critical deadlines for college applications and the like. He is a wonderful boy, but this becomes a problem again and again.

When we forget to ask him how much money he's carrying before he leaves MCI for a flight to California for the holidays, he winds up stranded at a bus station, broke. We move mountains to find a way to get his Argentine visa in New York City during a long weekend he has a vacation from school, only to have him show up in Manhattan without a passport and force us to start all over again with logistical gymnastics.

And therein is the second, related issue. What should be the consequence when he fails to meet obligations? Money still feels largely intangible to him, and he lives at boarding school, so grounding is of limited efficacy. No phone, no computer, no allowance—we try it all. But as always, the big question remains: how far would I ever let him fall? The ultimate consequence for Sammy—a boy without a US passport who could lose his visa if he doesn't do well—is so many million times harsher than the consequence for any of his peers in chemistry class.

Over the years this will be the issue I pray about more than any other.

The years to come are some of the most complicated and joyous of my life. My parents have it right when they say that I signed up for the hardest part of parenting—the teenage years. Sammy's adjustment to life in the United States goes better than anyone could have ever imagined, and he does so well that we have to remind ourselves—especially in the early months—of the stress we must not even realize he is under. Aside from the overarching challenges we face with teaching Sammy long-range goal setting and the nature of consequences when he makes mistakes, the majority of his problems seem to pattern themselves after the usual teenage variety: he loses more fleece jackets than I can count, he never has change for the dormitory Laundromat, and he is physically unable to wake up to his alarm clock.

But every so often, there are moments that remind me of his past.

The summer after he graduates from high school, three years after he first arrived in the United States and a few weeks before he leaves for a year of service work in Ecuador, we are at a Mexican restaurant in California and he is talking to me about chicken. "I had never eaten half a chicken before," he tells me about a meal he had the week before with a new friend. "And so I wanted to tell everyone on Facebook."

In the past three years, he has grown two feet taller—at least it looks like that, based on the old YouTube videos I have of him from 2006. Eating half a chicken and receiving regular, balanced meals subsidized with dorm pizzas that have tripled the calories of his Kenyan diet have surely helped.

"But then I stopped myself from posting about the chicken," he says. "Because I thought of people reading it back home in Kenya."

I feel momentarily blindsided by the turn this anecdote has taken. What I thought was a high school boy's calorie brag-fest has become something decidedly more somber. It is true, of course. The kids in Kenya are hungry that year. Crops are withering and animals are thin. We heard that even the orphanage's afternoon cup of weak, unsweetened tea had been cut out in recent months. We were all receiving an increasing number of pleas by phone and email from those we had left behind, asking for help and prayers. Understandably, Sammy takes these pleas the hardest, worrying deeply about what his peers are suffering through at home and what they think of his life now.

Sammy isn't the only one to edit his Facebook posts for his audience. Over the years Lara and I have been aware of this countless times. At my wedding in Argentina, for example, my husband and I made a point not to tag and post Sammy in endless photos while at the exotic locale. With so many of the Kenyan kids from Imani following our Facebook pages from afar, I knew the reach that "Sammy in a suit with opera singers" and "Sammy in the jungle hotel's infinity pool" would have, and I dreaded it. Countless other vacations, holidays, and days of "normal" life in the United States with him would reveal the same disconnect. "Sammy learning to drive a car"? "Sammy on yet another plane ride"? "Sammy with his new iPad"?

The conversation reminds me of how uncomfortable I am with the gap between our lives in the United States and the lives of his peers I care about in Kenya. Sammy—and the drastic 180 his life has taken in the past few years—embodies this wholeheartedly.

But not posting about what you had for lunch was a new level. In that moment at the Mexican restaurant, I feel once again how hard the life he has ahead of him will be to reconcile, and I only hope I will be there every step of the way to help him navigate it.

SAMMY

CHAPTER 14

During my junior year spring break, Claire gets married to an Argentine man named José, and I get to go to the wedding in Argentina for two weeks. This is my first time in any country outside of the United States or Kenya, and it is a very strange experience to take a plane from the Portland airport in Maine all the way to Buenos Aires. This time I know what the plane will be like, as I have been on others, and it makes the experience even more exciting than the first time.

Being in a whole new land and a whole new culture—again—is very weird. Claire and José pick me up at the airport, and it is the first time I have met José in person, as I have only seen him on Skype before. José is a soft-spoken, smart person, someone who really knows how to play music and to dance. Their wedding is the first wedding I have ever officially been to. In Kenya, I had never been invited to a wedding except my own parents' and a few occasions where I attended when people wanted me to videotape the wedding with Lara's camera. But then again, in Kenya, you don't really need to be invited to weddings. Whenever people in Kenya eat food in public, it means that everyone can take part.

At Claire's wedding, I meet all of Claire and Lara's friends from college. I am also introduced to Argentine beef for the first time, which is quite an experience—I love it. I learn all I can about Argentina, like that it has the widest avenue in the world, which takes three whole minutes to walk across. I can't imagine that in Kenya.

After the wedding, I go with Claire and José and their family and friends to Iguazu Falls, the widest waterfall in the world, a few hours by plane outside of Buenos Aires and near the Amazon.

Outside of what I see and experience, it is just amazing being there with Claire, José, Lara, and Lara's husband Louis. In Argentina, I am just so happy to have my whole five-person "Sammy family" in one place. It really feels like we are a unit, all together in person.

Since Lara's parents only live a few hours from Maine, it is really easy to get to know them, and from my first months in the United States I feel a part of their family, especially on holidays like Thanksgiving.

Since I've never celebrated Thanksgiving anywhere else, it is defined to me by Lara's family—even if they are vegetarians! Her parents, Frank and Melanie, and Lara's older brother Will, his wife Gabby, and their two kids John and Gracie, are always there. It is fun to be in a family with all sorts of people of all ages who accept me as a member of their clan and not just as a visitor.

On that first Thanksgiving sophomore year, I ask Lara if it is okay if I bring my friend Levan to her house with me. He is one of the postgraduate basketball players on the team I manage, and since he is from the country of Georgia, he doesn't have anywhere to go on Thanksgiving. At the time, Gracie is really small, and the first thing we do is tell Levan, who is huge, not to step on our little Gracie. When we Skype with Claire and José, we put Levan on the screen and Claire says, "He really *is* huge!"

We have so much fun that holiday weekend, and I remember the best thing we do is play foosball and have competitions to see who is better. I like being able to bring people to Lara's Thanksgiving just like I am another member of the family, and these friends become our guests. I do this again and again over the years.

After Thanksgiving, I am always excited for Christmas, and my first year I could not wait to see how people celebrate Christmas in the United States. I love to see all the family together and to spend so much time together celebrating. But even after all my years in the United States, I am still puzzled by the amount of gifts I see people giving each other. Although some places I go people tell me they don't give many gifts and prefer family time, in other places it seems that people get hundreds of gifts.

I think a lot about how different it is in Kenya, where people spend most of their time at Christmas cooking and eating. For Kenyans, the season is mostly about food, friends, and family, and everyone comes together to cook a chicken or slaughter a cow. At Imani, we ate meat with chapatti and rice and then ate that same meal again and again for a whole week. We all loved it. The schools also gave us more time off—a whole month—so we could travel far to visit our extended families, who sometimes lived days away by bus. My brother and I tried to see our family members at Christmas, but it was always difficult because we knew it put stress on my aunt to find and make food for us.

Even with all the presents at Christmas in the United States, I really miss those times.

During one of these school vacations, I meet a really amazing person who, little by little, becomes like a brother to me. Brian

Williams is the founder of an organization called Think Kindness, and he goes around the country promoting kindness. I spend a vacation or two with his family, and Brian begins to take care of me, calling me up at school every now and again to see how I am doing.

Throughout my three years at school, what I learn more than anything is that whenever someone considers you family, you are family, and that's all that matters.

When Lara and Claire take me in, even though we don't have official titles for one another, we are a family.

After three years at MCI, I am about to graduate. It feels like I have just started my new life in America, but in reality a lot of time has passed. I have met many people over the years; some have become friends and some have become family.

I apply to a lot of colleges in my senior year at MCI, but I also try for a different type of program called Global Citizen Year (GCY), which is an organization that places high school graduates in developing countries to live and work for a year before college. It gives them a chance to learn, grow, and become better leaders and better people before they start university. Most of all, it gives teenagers a new perspective on the world, and I am excited to be a part of it.

Claire is a supporter of the program and told me about it when I was a sophomore to see if I might be interested someday. As soon as I am old enough, I apply. I am thrilled to be accepted, and I even get a 75 percent scholarship. However, I still need to raise seven thousand dollars. This is hard, but doing this program is my dream, and I have to succeed.

But before I can even think about Global Citizen Year, I have to graduate! One of the requirements MCI has is a senior project, which is a long-term project each student must complete that either helps them learn more about a subject or has a positive impact on the community around MCI. Although I'm not sure what I want to do, I know that any project I do will have to help two of the homes I now have in my heart: Maine and Kenya. What I want most of all is for people in my Maine home to have a little experience of what I went through living in the orphanage. I also dream of helping people in Kenya by giving them a taste of what Maine Central Institute is all about.

I start to talk to some people to brainstorm ideas, and during one of these chats, Brian Williams of Think Kindness gives me the idea to see if I can collect one thousand pairs of shoes to send to Imani. I think this is a perfect way to bring together my school, Maine Central Institute, with my home at Imani, through the running programs I did in both places. I remember how much getting my first pair of running shoes from Claire and Lara affected me, and I want to give that feeling of joy to other kids at Imani. I call my effort the Kindness Project and quickly recruit a group of other students and advisors to help me. I call them the Kindness Crew, and I make them responsible for helping me organize shoe drives and put together a 5K race—all with the goal of collecting shoes and getting the money we need to ship them to Kenya.

Another important part of the Kindness Project is inspired by Brian. Like him, I start giving speeches to people on how they can include random acts of kindness in their daily lives. I ask people in the community to help me recognize people around the school who perform random acts of kindness on a daily basis, and we seek out businesses in the Pittsfield community to reward such good-hearted individuals. I then recognize these individuals in front of the whole school so they can serve as a continual inspiration for everyone else.

From the first speech I give about the project to the school, I am surprised and honored by the support that I see, with even more of it coming from the students than the teachers and staff members. By the end of the campaign, I have collected three thousand pairs of shoes—three times my goal!—and my senior project has become a way to truly connect the people I love in Maine with the people I love at Imani. I appear in local news programs and newspapers, and everyone at MCI is proud to be involved.

This experience helps me realize that, as humans, we always have opportunities to help one another. Yes, we do need to work to make money to support our lives, but what is the real value of living if your neighbor is suffering, or if your family member or friend is in pain?

I knew about how important it is to help others, especially given all the people who came to the orphanage over the years, but when I begin to make it part of my own life I am amazed to see how much people are willing to sacrifice their time, money, and anything they have to help a project succeed. Even though the experience is really hard—especially when it comes to organizing a 5K race—I am proud to have led the project. I owe a lot to the Kindness Crew, for without them I could never have finished it. Although I like thinking I am helping my friends at home at Imani, I know the real reason I am doing it is because I need to. Helping should not be about how it makes me feel.

Soon it is time to graduate. This is one of the sweetest moments of my life, but it is also very hard. I have come to make Maine my home, and I have made amazing friends: Alena, my best friend who always helped me, Avery, Franci, and many more. My teachers have been so kind to me and have never treated me like just an "African kid." Instead, they have treated me like one of their own and have helped me the whole way.

Sadly, Lara and Claire are both unable to fly the weekend of my graduation. Claire is very sick, and Lara is giving birth to her baby in California. It is very hard, but I am happy to have Lara's brother

Will, his wife Gabby, and their two kids drive up for the event. Lara and Claire get to be on Skype with Will for the ceremonies, and they laugh and say that it looks like the graduation is really "The Sammy Show." It is true that the teachers talk about me and my senior project a lot on the stage, even making kindness the theme of the school's work for the next year. I am so pleased that even though I came to MCI so confused and lost, in the end the school is proud enough to talk about me at graduation.

My last day at MCI is very bittersweet. Saying goodbye to everyone, taking pictures in our gowns, and being honored together for our accomplishments is a wonderful experience. At the ceremony, I am recognized as a leader, and I feel happy about all that I have contributed to the MCI community.

It has been a great life, but it is time to move on.

After graduation, Brian invites me to Reno, Nevada, to spend the whole summer interning with him at Think Kindness. I also have to work with Claire and Lara to get my visa for Ecuador (where I am being sent with Global Citizen Year!) and to raise the money I need to participate in the program. I am so excited about Ecuador and am eager to learn my fourth language, Spanish. I am thrilled to think about the new country, the new culture, and the new experiences that lie ahead of me. Just like when I came to the United States, I do not know how it will be, but I know I am ready.

Over the summer, I complete my internship alongside Brian and another Think Kindness volunteer, Brianna. I also go to California a couple times to see Claire when she flies into town, as well as Lara and Louis and their new baby, Oscar.

On my last trip before I go to Ecuador, Lara gives me an incredible surprise. She has baked a cake to congratulate me for everything! It is the first cake anyone has ever baked for me, and I can't believe she has done that. It is so delicious. However, that last day in the United States is still an incredibly hard day. I say goodbye to Claire's parents, Barb and Lance, and then Lara takes me to the airport. I feel terrible because I don't know how many months it will be until I see my "Sammy family" again.

I am leaving the United States, not sure when I will return, and I cannot help but think about all the things that have happened since I first came here and all the changes I have gone through. I arrived in the United States as a boy without a family, and I leave a man with a great one. I now have a family who will take care of me, a family who will love me all the time, a family who will yell at me if I do something wrong, and a family who will celebrate with me when I do something great. This is what I am most pleased with having accomplished, and I cherish it. I pray day in and day out that I will never lose it.

At the airport, when I get out of the car, Lara starts yelling at me out the car window. "Be careful! Call me!" And all those kinds of things that a mom says to her son. If Claire were here, she would be saying the same things, and I feel so proud and happy.

Eighteen hours later I arrive in Quito, Ecuador. The host family I am going to stay with comes to pick me up at the airport, and it is immediately very funny to me that I have almost no Spanish language experience. Claire and José have taught me a few things, but the only words I can remember are "Hi!" and "I don't speak Spanish." My host parents start speaking to me and I just sit there, nodding, having no idea what they are talking about. From their hands, I try to guess what they are saying—where I am supposed to sleep and what time I am supposed to be where.

On my first morning in Ecuador, my host father, Jorge, wakes me up and shows me where to take a shower. After I get dressed, he takes me to the kitchen and gives me a breakfast of empanadas, which I love. Then he takes me on a bus and shows me where to jump off when the bus passes a particular statue and where to walk to get to the language institute I will be studying at. I try to remember everything, but it takes a few tries until I can repeat the directions back to him correctly.

At the institute, I am thrilled that there are Global Citizen Year employees who speak English. After my host father leaves, I go to my first Spanish class with a lovely lady named Sofia. That first class is extremely hard, because Sofia speaks in Spanish and only uses English if it is really, really important.

Soon it is coffee break time, and I am exhausted after two hours of listening to a teacher say things I can't understand. At break, I begin to meet other students from different countries like Switzerland and Germany. After some tea and cookies, I have to go back to class, even though I dread it.

For two more hours, the teacher talks on and on about things I don't understand. I do feel like I am learning, though. I learn to say "I am" and "you are," and I start to understand what the verb *to be* is all about. It is challenging, but I keep my mind to it.

The teacher tells me I have to buy some things, like a bigger notebook. At least I think that's what she says.

Soon all of the Global Citizen Year fellows arrive in Ecuador. It is amazing to meet this smart, engaging group of students so eager to learn—students just like me who have wanted to come to Ecuador to spend their time volunteering and learning about the culture. I do feel like a bit of an outsider, but at least I am no longer the only one feeling that way in Ecuador. The students all are feeling like I do to some extent.

Living with my Quito family is a new experience for me. They are a middle-class family, and every day they pack me a lunch to take to school. At night we have dinner, and they ask how my day was and how everything is going. Claire and Lara have been my family for the last four years, but we didn't all live together in one house. In reality, I haven't lived in a house with parents since I was ten years old, so this is a marvel.

On top of that, the Quito family is really helpful in teaching me Spanish. At dinner, I sit with my mother and she tells me things. "This is a cup. This is bread. This is coffee." She shows me some things around the house and teaches me what their words are in Spanish, and that's how I learn the basics. The only word I find that seems related to Swahili is *mesa*, or "table." Other than that, though, this fourth language seems so different from the others I know.

I make friends quickly with the other fellows, and together we decide to explore and get to know Ecuador better. I love seeing more of Quito and learn all about the difference between Old Quito and New Quito. Most people live in New Quito, but all the great, old buildings are in the old part of the city.

After a month of language and culture training in Quito, we are told it is time to move on to the communities we will be living in and helping for the rest of the year. The names of the communities are all written on pieces of paper inside balloons that we have to pop. My paper says Salinas.

One of my closest friends in Global Citizen Year is a boy named Canaan, and he is placed in a community near me. Canaan is actually from Ethiopia, Kenya's northern neighbor, and though he was raised mostly in the United States, we share a lot. A girl named Kip will also be near me in the same province.

As we learn about the community, I realize it is an Afro-Ecuadorian community, which doesn't make me that happy. I had purposely not wanted to be in an African community, even requesting that

Global Citizen Year not place me in their program in Senegal before I was assigned to Ecuador. Being placed in an Afro-Ecuadorian community doesn't sound like it will be a new cultural experience for me. I end up being very wrong about that, but I didn't know it at the time.

All the kids going to my province meet at the bus, and we start out on the four-hour bus ride. I am getting nervous, and I know I am not the only one. When we arrive at the bus terminal, I see that some host parents have started showing up. I see joy on the faces of many of the volunteers and families. After all, it is an exciting thing to meet the family you will live with for nine whole months.

After twenty minutes, my family hasn't shown up, and my nerves are getting worse. Then I see a black lady walking toward me. Since I am the only volunteer still waiting who is serving in an Afro-Ecuadorian community, I know she must be there for me. She greets the Global Citizen Year staff member and introduces herself to me. Then she says she is in a hurry. I quickly say goodbye to my friends and follow this woman, who I learn is named Capu. She says she is excited to get to know me, but I'm not sure, because her facial expression does not say the same thing.

We immediately get in a taxi with all my stuff, and then we stop at a gas station, where we get into another car, and inside that car she introduces me to her husband Diego, my host father. There are two boys in the car as well, two of my new host brothers—Diego, thirteen, and Herman, eighteen. The first thing that sticks out to me is that my mother has married a man who isn't black. This is the first time I have ever seen that. When they tell me the car is their own, I realize this family must not be as poor as I thought.

We drive for a while through a really beautiful area, and then we enter the little community of Salinas. It is really hot, and all the concrete buildings everywhere make it hotter. On the streets, everyone seems to be sitting on the stoops, and I can see that almost everyone is black. It does not seem like the cultural experience I was looking for.

I live with Capu and her family for one week, and she shows me where I will be working and introduces me to people throughout the community. I find out that there are members of the national football team who come from the community, and I think that is pretty cool.

After a week of getting to know people, I feel relieved that I have been placed in the community I have. Everyone seems to accept me so easily as one of them, and not one person thinks I look different. The first weekend I am there, a big festival and a fireworks show takes place, and at the show I meet some kids my age who live in the community. Again and again, I feel that I come from the same place these people do.

Everyone is really interested that I am from Africa. They call Africa their motherland and try to associate themselves with the continent as much as they can. As soon as I tell someone from the community I am from Africa, I become a cooler person to them, and they immediately ask me questions about the music, the food, or the culture of Africa. It is very different from Maine. I take it as a fun chance to teach and expose people to what the real Africa is like.

I try to be as realistic as possible whenever I explain where I came from. A lot of people immediately say things like, "Isn't Africa where a lot of people don't have food and are always hungry?" I say, "Yes, for some people in Africa." Then I say that I've heard of some parts of Ecuador where people don't have food or water and no one has clothes and everyone is backwards. Then they laugh and understand what I am trying to show them. Yes, there is hunger in Africa, there is drought, but it's not every place, and it's not something that every person faces.

I also try to help them see that the media is really changing the way people are thinking about Africa. I say, "You know how some journalists have taken pictures of those Ecuadorian tribes with the painted faces that live in the forest?" I point out that a Kenyan who sees that picture will think all of Ecuador is like that, when it's not. Things are not always what people think they are.

I let the Ecuadorians know that what they see on the news is what the media wants to show—the most shocking things. People aren't seeing that Kenya is developing and is trying to get ahead and elevate itself.

During my time in Salinas, I have a few different jobs, or apprenticeships. First, I work with youth in some social development programs. For example, I give talks about sexual reproductive health and lead games to help people learn what I have taught. I also organize talks on alcoholism and on other issues that affect youth development in the area. One of my most successful programs is a computer literacy program that I start teaching at a cultural center. A range of people start coming—not just youth—and I am pleased to see how it really picks up over the months.

I also work on a dance therapy program for senior citizens and people with disabilities. We go from house to house checking people's health, making sure they are eating well and staying healthy. We make sure the adults are doing some exercises as well, and we always integrate some dancing to music they really love.

Living in the small community of Salinas teaches me some important life lessons, and I learn a lot about cultural acceptance and not making judgments of others. It isn't always easy, though.

For a long time I think that my host mother is really mean to my brothers and me because she just yells at us all the time, and I don't like it at all. To avoid her, I go to work and stay out until really late, like 8:30 or 9:00 p.m., and just come home to eat and sleep. When I arrived, I also felt like people didn't appreciate me because

I am black. Usually the volunteers who come to the community are from the United States, the United Kingdom, or Germany, and they have blonde hair and blue eyes. Since I am not that, I think my host mother doesn't like me, and I reason that's why she is always shouting. I feel uncomfortable in the house but decide not to tell anyone about it, and whenever people ask how I am doing, I say I am fine.

It is at this time that I know I need a visit from my real family—my "Sammy family"—and I am so happy that Claire, Lara, Louis, José, and baby Oscar come to Ecuador to see me. When they come to Salinas, they spend a lot of time talking to Capu and trying to understand some of the problems in our relationship. Capu is complaining that I am not doing things according to her rules, and as I hear her complain more, I start to tell Lara and Claire, "I just do not want to be here."

As Lara and Claire are saying I have a good host mother, I am saying I have the worst host mother in the world. This is when Lara and Claire sit me down and explain something to me about mothers that I have never known. They tell me that after talking with Capu, they can see that she really is trying to take care of me. They explain that Capu does care, and she is trying to keep me out of trouble. Her rules are strict, but she is treating me like a son and working hard to make sure I am living a safe, productive way. It is not easy for her to follow every little thing I do and to correct me over and over until I learn to do it right.

Lara and Claire tell me it would be easier for Capu to just let me do whatever I want, but she knows that wouldn't be best for me as a man. They explain that mothers who care for you like Capu are more right than I can understand in the moment, and I need to learn to obey her even when it is hard. They try to make me understand more about Capu as a person: she is very busy, she works very late, and her husband comes home only every other month because he is a truck driver, so she is doing things all alone. They talk to me like an adult and tell me that I need to learn to look at things in an adult way—to cut her some slack and see things as they really are.

I haven't realized the reality that my host mother is basically a single mother who works a hard job in a chicken factory to provide for her family. She has four boys in the house, including me, and worries about how to provide for everyone. She washes her sons' clothes not because she has time or because they are too young to do it themselves but because she doesn't want them to ruin their clothes, as she is so worried about not having the money to pay for new ones. She works hard, but sometimes her kids don't do well in school and she has to go in to talk to their teachers. She is trying so hard to do everything, and her boys don't always help her. I realize I have to learn to understand her and to look at things from her perspective.

Little by little, it works. I start coming home earlier so that we have time to talk after dinner. Sometimes we talk for hours, and I look at the clock and don't know where the time has gone. Through these talks, I get to understand her pains—how hard it is for her as a mother that her kids don't always treat her well or listen to her, and why she feels she always has to yell to be heard. I start to see that if I hadn't opened my mind to her problems and seen whatever was going through her head, I would never have grown close to her.

That is when I find a friend in Capu and a woman who really cares about me. Since she is black like me, she jokes that I am the son she carried in her belly who was accidentally born in Kenya!

I realize that sometimes we need to open up to people, understand their pains, and see what they're going through in order to get to know them better and truly become friends. If it wasn't for Lara and Claire visiting me and opening my mind, I would not have had a wonderful experience in Ecuador.

Ecuador opens my eyes to the real kindness and humanity of strangers. It isn't the first time in my life I have seen this, but it is a time when I see this kindness come from people who don't know my story. In Ecuador, they see me as a foreigner—a rich one on a fancy American program—and yet they still give of themselves to support me. In many ways, they look at me like I looked at Claire and Lara all those years ago in Kenya. I meet people who don't know me but want to help me. People with whom I want to be friends, and people who want to invite me into their families. I meet friends who will stay with me my whole life.

In Ecuador, I open my mind to a new world.

CLAIRE

CHAPTER 15

The decision to bring Sammy to the United States was not made lightly, and it didn't come without a host of real concerns. Given Sammy's incredibly successful transition to the United States, thankfully most of those concerns never come to fruition. One, however, never goes away.

From the beginning, I worried about some of the negative long-term consequences for him, culturally and psychologically, of the objectively wonderful opportunity of leaving a Kenyan orphanage to come to a US boarding school. I never wanted him to feel he had to hide his past, nor did I want him distancing himself too far from the concerns of his peers at home in Kenya. And so, the year Sammy first started at MCI, I told him about a wonderful program for US high school graduates that I believed might be a way to try to bridge the two different worlds he had lived in. Sammy leaped on the idea, and by the time he graduated from high school, he was thrilled to start a year serving as a volunteer in a poor community in Ecuador with a program called Global Citizen Year.

Lara and I had long discussed the fact that Sammy would face a time in life when he would have to move from being someone who has been helped for so long to someone who is providing that help to others, and his time with Global Citizen Year in Ecuador helps him do just that.

When we visit him there, where he lives in a rural community with his host family, enjoying relationships with international friends who share his interest in helping the world, I know it is right.

And then there is the question of the next step. His dream is to attend a US college, but this proves a trickier beast. Without state residency, all twenty-nine colleges he applies to are incredibly pricey, and even with the scholarships he is afforded, he is staring down six figures in loans. Without the guarantee of a US work visa after graduation, this is a terrifying burden to take on, and not a wise gamble.

He wants to think about it, he says. And more importantly, he needs to spend some time back in Kenya first, as he has visited only once in his years away. Lara and I tell him we love him and will always support him wherever he is. We want him to find the country that he is best fit to live in long term, and the best school for him to reach his dreams.

But letting him go is one of the hardest things that happens to me.

In the end, my subconscious overrides, and I make a logistical error that seems to mean something somewhere. At the airport in Quito, he can't get on the plane because I booked him a flight on the wrong day. For the thousandth time that year, the Global Citizen Year staff generously overlooks our scrambling, unpracticed mothering from thousands of miles away, and they step in and help Sammy negotiate this new twist.

"It's like you don't want me back in Kenya!" He laughs into the cell phone from Quito as we frantically solve the nightmare I created. I have booked thousands of flights over the years and serve as my family's de facto travel agent. I have never done this.

I cringe at his words. And so I turn a joke into something serious, and I say again what Lara and I have always said, and what we mean so fiercely it makes me weep.

"Sammy, I want you to be wherever you want to be in the world. Kenya, the United States, Ecuador—it doesn't matter to me where you want to live your life. I simply want you to be where you—and God—want you to be. But wherever it is, I want for you a life that is one million times better than the one you knew as a child. That is my dream, and that's the dream I fight for each day."

He'll come back, he says. And he gets on the plane.

SAMMY

CHAPTER 16

I write the last words of this story on a plane in the clouds. After a year in Ecuador and more than four years away from Kenya, I am going home. At least for a time.

My stay in Ecuador has changed me, and as I look back on what I have done and what I want to do, I know that this experience was a moment like no other.

In Ecuador, I found many mothers. People who wanted the best for me and who sacrificed some of their time to see that I took the next step. During the year, I often walked around with my Ecuadorian host family as they talked about their family. They would introduce me to relatives and tell me, "This is my aunt" or "This is my uncle." When they did this, I felt how badly I wanted that. I wanted to have a mother next to me and a father by my side.

But for me, that is not possible in the traditional way.

With time, I grew close to my host mother, and I understood that she didn't look at me like a rich American or a poor orphan, but she looked at me as one of her sons. As part of this role, she helped me realize everything that Claire and Lara have been for me over the last seven years and what a special relationship we have.

When people ask me who Claire and Lara are, I don't know what to say. "Guardian. Aunt. Mother. Big sister. I don't know," I tell them. They're just my family. They're my friends. They are Claire and Lara. They are the people who brought me from the dust and gave me a life.

In Ecuador, I found a sense of ownership of who I am and what I represent. Before I arrived, I was scared of having my goals and ideas rejected as impossible. When I was accepted to Global Citizen Year, I didn't know whether people would accept me as a young African male coming to volunteer. I worried they would think I was doing something negative or that someone like me couldn't help.

Then when Global Citizen Year told me I would be volunteering in an Afro-Ecuadorian community, it brought out all my worst fears. I feared rejection simply because I too was African. I wasn't a common gringo, a white person with blue eyes and blonde hair; therefore, I wasn't the type who volunteered and helped people. I was scared to be an African among Africans. In the end, when I realized I could really help people just by being myself and that my presence there actually changed what people think of twenty-first-century Africans, I found a feeling of ownership. And that is why I am so proud of and happy for what I have done.

Ecuador also helped me think about where I would be had I not made the journey across the ocean years ago. The Sammy who left Maine had, in many ways, moved beyond his past. He had gone to high school, he had overcome prejudice, he had gotten good grades, he had worked hard to help his peers at home. He was an MVP and a team captain in two sports. The Sammy who came to Ecuador, and who is leaving Ecuador now, is a Sammy I have much higher expectations for.

My future goals are simple. First, I want to go to college. College for me is yet another second chance in life. The experiences I have there will not only transform who I am but also help me to give back and use my own education to help children who are less fortunate. I am sick and tired of seeing so many people ride around in nice cars and lead a great life when there are still children on the streets with nowhere to go, and children who still sleep in trash cans. In my life, I want to be able to give those children a second chance, a third chance, a fourth chance—just like I have been given.

Another goal for me is to rebuild my relationship with my biological family in Kenya. Having my sister, my brother, my aunt, and my cousins near is something I miss. During all the years I have been gone, it has been hard to keep in contact, and this has saddened me. There have been times I have sat down and cried. When we do talk, it is often about money, sadly. I know the situations they are in and I've gone through them myself, so I understand. But I am a student and I cannot provide. Yet.

When I think of my little sister Bethi, I feel the huge weight of leaving her alone at her weakest. My father died when she was a day old, and my mother left when she was four. Now she is fifteen, and I have seen her only a few times in a dozen years. I think to myself that I will do everything I can for her, just like Claire and Lara have done for me. Even though my aunt has taken good care of her throughout the years, I want to make sure to be there for her in the future. At the very least, I owe her that.

And that is a vow I have taken.

Most of all, I am motivated to succeed as a thank-you to all those who have helped me throughout my life. The list is long, since my life has been filled with people who have showed me endless kindness—bathing me, clothing me, feeding me, loving me. I owe these people my success in life. First, there was my mother's friend, the one who saw me, my brother, and my sister on the street and decided to call our extended family. Then there was my aunt Lydia Njeri, who took us in when no one else would. Then there was Imani Children's Home. And then there were Claire and Lara, who provided me with a new life. Later, at MCI, Global Citizen Year, and Think Kindness, so many others came forward to help me. All these people have sacrificed of themselves to get me where I am today, and I know I now stand on their shoulders. I take all of them and all of their expectations back to Kenya with me.

I look out the plane, and I watch for the red dirt road.

ACKNOWLEDGMENTS

Claire

Books are behemoths, and no one writes one alone. Here are some of the people who graciously helped on this one.

To all the incredible adults who have worked tirelessly to improve the lives of the orphanage's children: the Very Reverend, Eunice, Francis, Cucu, Prisca, Priscilla, Virginia, Eve, Zach, Paul and Stephanie, Brian and Katie T., Brian W., Jonathan and Jessica, Michael and Emilee, Kelly, Renee, and all the elders and administrators at the orphanage over the years.

To the troublemakers, the crazy ones, the ones who taught me about parenting when mothering seemed the furthest thing from my mind—you are too many to count. A few: Chula, Mwaniki, Rhoda (Big and Little), Faith, Mwai, James, Hannah Banana, Simon, Caroline, Jane, Ephantus, and Edwin. Oh, Edwin.

To the 2006 blog readers—the originals—who made me believe someone might ever want to hear any part of this strange story.

To Biz Stone and my many amazing colleagues at Twitter over the years. My, the places we've gone.

To the Otero Girls, for being the best cheerleaders a two-dollar check can buy.

To Andrea, Twila, Lindsay, Janelle, Cheryl, Jessica, and the entire Revell team, for finding a home and shaping this book into what it could be. And to Esther, a force.

To Byrd, an incredible advocate and kindhearted one.

To Don, for taking on one more thing in a huge season.

To all who read the many drafts of this text and provided critical commentary: Mom, Dad, Lara, Louis, José, and Amalia.

To everyone who has opened their hearts and homes to take in Sammy: Team MCI (Clint and Declan, among others), Team GCY (Abby, Eileen, Maria, and more), Team Reno (including Brian's entire family), Melanie, Frank, Gabby, Will, Dad, Mom, and many more.

To Lara, who sparked this journey and made it worthwhile. When we are old and gray, I will think of us on a dingy street corner in Phnom Penh at five in the morning, desperately in search of spotty wireless three minutes before a deadline.

To Sammy, as you find your future, may you remember this past.

To José, whom I found along the way. Our improbable tour is just beginning.

To baby Díaz-Ortiz, for whom we've waited for so long. Please don't come a week early, so Mamá can launch this book.

Sammy

During the long writing process, I have had so many people give of their time to make this book a success. I would like to thank everyone who contributed to seeing this book in print, but I would like to particularly thank the following people for their help on it and their support in my life.

To my sister Bethi, for being a constant motivator during the process (in absentia). Striving for the best for you gives me encouragement every day. And to Muriithi.

Given everything that has happened in my life, I always remember that things happen for a reason and that God has a plan. I also believe there are two sides to every story and that my mother would not have left us if she did not have a concrete reason for doing so. One day I hope to know that reason. Until that happens, I know I will never be truly at peace.

To the children's home, its sponsors, and its management. I want to thank you for how you changed my life. To the founder, the managers, and the matrons (current and former), for being caring mothers and fathers to me. You taught me more than I can fully express. Thank you.

To Global Citizen Year and its inspiring founder, Abby Falik, who gave me help, resources, and time while I was in the program and also writing this book. Thank you. Further thanks to the Global Citizen Year Ecuador Program, its director, Eileen, the entire 2013 cohort, and its partners, the Experiment in International Living.

To Marilene and Miriam, for everything you did to help me. To Maria Christina and Olga, for time and help during the writing process. To Canaan, for peer feedback, critiques, and essential help on chapter outlines.

To Think Kindness and its founder, Brian Williams, my other big brother. Thank you for brotherly advice and a whole lot of kindness over the years.

Thank you to Declan, for giving me new perspectives each and every day with intelligent words and kind direction.

Ultimately, this book would not have been a reality without the major help and support of the "Sammy family," which includes

Claire and José Díaz-Ortiz, Lara Vogel, Louis Dorval, baby Oscar Dorval, and soon-to-be baby Díaz-Ortiz. Claire, you are like the backbone of this book, an editor and fine-tuner of the highest degree. Thank you. Lara, Louis, and José, thank you for your encouragements and edits as well during this process. Throughout this book—and the last eight years—you have been there to help me when I needed it, to direct me as a parent should when things were not perfect, and to celebrate with me when all was well.

Thank you all.

ABOUT HOPE RUNS

Hope Runs is a nonprofit organization still operating in Kenya today, serving the needs of the orphanage where Sammy grew up. It currently provides in-orphanage athletic programming and college scholarships to orphanage graduates who successfully complete secondary school and seek to pursue a university education. Many of the children featured in this book have gone on to graduate from a university using such funds. Proceeds from this book go to support the ongoing work of Hope Runs.

To learn more about Hope Runs or to make a tax-deductible donation, go to www.HopeRuns.org.

ABOUT THE AUTHORS

Claire Díaz-Ortiz is an author, speaker, and technology innovator who has been named one of the 100 Most Creative People in Business by *Fast Company*. Claire was an early employee at Twitter, where she was hired to lead social innovation, and where she still works today.

In Claire's work, she has been called everything from "the woman who got the pope on Twitter" (*Wired*) and "Twitter's pontiff recruitment chief" (*Washington Post*) to a "force for good" (*Forbes*) and "one of the most generous people in social media" (*Fast Company*).

Claire is the author of several books, including *Twitter for Good: Change the World One Tweet at a Time* and *Greater Expectations: Succeed (and Stay Sane) in an On-Demand, All-Access, Always-On Age*. She is a frequent international speaker on social media, business, and innovation and writes a popular business blog at www. ClaireDiazOrtiz.com. She is also a LinkedIn Influencer, one of several hundred global leaders chosen to provide original content for the LinkedIn platform.

Claire holds an MBA from Oxford University, where she was a Skoll Foundation Scholar for Social Entrepreneurship, and has a BA and an MA in anthropology from Stanford University.

She is the cofounder of Hope Runs, a nonprofit organization operating in AIDS orphanages in Kenya. She has appeared widely in major television and print news sources such as CNN, BBC, *Time*, *Newsweek*, the *New York Times*, the *Washington Post*, *Fortune*, *Forbes*, *Wired*, and many others.

Read more about her at www.ClaireDiazOrtiz.com or on Twitter via @claire.

Samuel Ikua Gachagua was born in rural Kenya in 1992. After losing his parents at a young age, he struggled to survive until he was placed in an orphanage in Nyeri, Kenya, a move that saved his life. In 2006, two women came to live in his orphanage for a year and start a nonprofit organization, Hope Runs. Soon after, Sammy had his first experiences of videography—which would become one of his passions—during a photo shoot for *Runner's World* at the orphanage. Since that time, he has always had a camera or two in his pocket.

In 2009, he received a scholarship to Maine Central Institute, granting him a rare US visa and the chance to begin his sophomore year of high school in the United States, under the guardianship of the women who had lived in his orphanage years earlier and had searched far and wide for a way to bring him to the United States for a better education. He graduated from high school in 2012 and spent a year as a fellow with Global Citizen Year, a nonprofit organization in Ecuador, where he led service projects in rural communities and learned his fourth language. He is currently eager to pursue a college education.

Sammy is an up-and-coming motivational speaker and has been featured prominently in the award-winning documentary *The Roots of Happiness*, as well as in local print and television media in Maine. This is his first book.

Find him on Twitter via @sammyikua or at www.sammyikua.com.

Founded by Claire Díaz-Ortiz and Lara Vogel,
Hope Runs is a nonprofit organization that uses
running to empower AIDS orphans in Kenya with the
tools of personal health, social entrepreneurship,
and education.

To donate or find out more information, please visit
HOPERUNS.ORG

"A searingly honest story of one woman's awakening from a coma after her baby's birth—and her long road back. . . . *Unforgettable.*"

—ERIC METAXAS, *New York Times* bestselling author

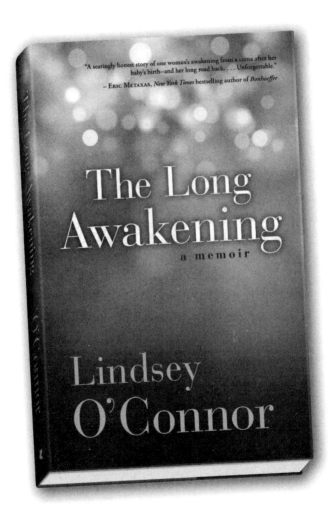

"A beautiful, heartbreaking,
grace-soaked story."

–SHAUNA NIEQUIST, author of *Cold Tangerines,
Bittersweet*, and *Bread & Wine*

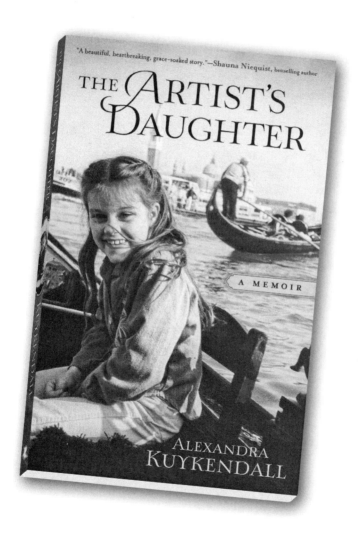

"A beautiful, heartbreaking, grace-soaked story."—Shauna Niequist, bestselling author

THE ARTIST'S
DAUGHTER

A MEMOIR

ALEXANDRA
KUYKENDALL